Out of the spiral of conflict

Andrea Hartmann-Piraudeau

Out of the spiral of conflict

Our conflicts - And how we solve them

 Springer

Andrea Hartmann-Piraudeau
Stuttgart, Germany

ISBN 978-3-658-39778-4   ISBN 978-3-658-39779-1   (eBook)
https://doi.org/10.1007/978-3-658-39779-1

© The Editor(s) (if applicable) and The Author(s), under exclusive licence to Springer Fachmedien Wiesbaden GmbH, part of Springer Nature 2022
This book is a translation of the original German edition „Raus aus der Konfliktspirale" by Hartmann-Piraudeau, Andrea, published by Springer Fachmedien Wiesbaden GmbH in 2021. The translation was done with the help of artificial intelligence (machine translation by the service DeepL.com). A subsequent human revision was done primarily in terms of content, so that the book will read stylistically differently from a conventional translation. Springer Nature works continuously to further the development of tools for the production of books and on the related technologies to support the authors.
This work is subject to copyright. All rights are solely and exclusively licensed by the Publisher, whether the whole or part of the material is concerned, specifically the rights of translation, reprinting, reuse of illustrations, recitation, broadcasting, reproduction on microfilms or in any other physical way, and transmission or information storage and retrieval, electronic adaptation, computer software, or by similar or dissimilar methodology now known or hereafter developed.
The use of general descriptive names, registered names, trademarks, service marks, etc. in this publication does not imply, even in the absence of a specific statement, that such names are exempt from the relevant protective laws and regulations and therefore free for general use.
The publisher, the authors, and the editors are safe to assume that the advice and information in this book are believed to be true and accurate at the date of publication. Neither the publisher nor the authors or the editors give a warranty, expressed or implied, with respect to the material contained herein or for any errors or omissions that may have been made. The publisher remains neutral with regard to jurisdictional claims in published maps and institutional affiliations.

This Springer imprint is published by the registered company Springer Fachmedien Wiesbaden GmbH, part of Springer Nature.
The registered company address is: Abraham-Lincoln-Str. 46, 65189 Wiesbaden, Germany

Contents

1 **Introduction** 1

2 **The Nature of Conflicts** 5
   2.1 Constructive Conflicts 6
   2.2 Destructive/Dysfunctional Conflicts 8
   2.3 Hot and Cold Conflicts 11
   2.4 The Escalation of Conflicts 15
   2.5 The Aura of Conflict 19

3 **Conflict Types** 25
   3.1 Everyone Is Different: Personalities 26
   3.2 What Type of Conflict Am I? 36
   3.3 What Types of Conflict Resolution Are There? 45

4 **The Spiral of Conflict** 57
   4.1 Change in Thinking 58
   4.2 Change in Feeling 62
   4.3 Change in the Will 64

5 **Conflict Resolution** 71
   5.1 Self Clarification 72
   5.2 Understanding the Others 79
   5.3 Making Peace 85

1

Introduction

> **Example**
>
> The door slams shut. With her fists clenched in her pockets, Nina trudges into the garden. Her heart races, she breathes loudly. The skin of her face tenses, her molars clenched. A carousel of thoughts starts in your head. "I've had enough, always I'm supposed to give in, not with me… Now I'm going to go in and tell Johannes I'm sick of it… now I'm going to think about me… He'll see where this is going… soon he'll be alone, he won't even need to see the kids… then he'll regret it…". Nina's inner merry-go-round spins faster. Tender voices slow down the ride: "… Well, maybe it's better we get along again… Think of the children… you are a good team… you love him… he doesn't mean it… put yourself in his place". Often the inner peace messengers managed to stop the merry-go-round. With each argument, however, came fewer. This time your voices are thin- they are driven away- the merry-go-round continues to spin. Nina is in the spiral of conflict.
>
> "This can't go on, I'm about to burst… If he looks at me with his fake smile one more time, I'll go for his throat". Martin sits in the team meeting. He looks the same as always. The suit is on, freshly shaved, the folder in front of him on the table, the papers sorted. Inside, the volcano is about to erupt. He's warm. His veins at the temples are pulsing. His fingers are cold and sticky, his chest tightens, his heart pounds hard. He can no longer hear what his colleague is presenting. "Never again, will I work with him… I'll flatten him… He'll see… I've always known what a jerk he is, enough is enough… the barrel is full". The meeting ends, Martin wordlessly leaves the room. He sits down in his office, door closed, headphones on. His thoughts are racing. Martin is in a spiral of conflict.
>
> Tanja cries. It's all too much for her. First the death of her parents and now this. We stick together, that's what they had sworn at her mother's grave. "Luckily we have each other". "How good that there are three of you" – the funeral card said – "Siblings are important, especially when things get difficult in life". And now this. It's been going on for weeks – arguments about money, old books, photo albums, cemetery maintenance. Nothing is simple anymore. We don't talk anymore, only write. The brother has left the WhatsApp group. When an email arrives, Tanja's chest tightens, she looks at the subject and has to overcome herself to open it. When she does, her fingers tremble, tears shoot into her eyes and a large lump sticks in her throat. Her legs feel weak, she feels dizzy, the letters blur. Reproach again. "That's so mean, how can she say I've always been favored by Papa…they might as well ask themselves why Papa was so hard on them, they weren't particularly nice either… Calling me a spoiled brat is just mean… I certainly won't give in, if you talk to me like that I'll draw other sides too…". Tanja's cheeks turn red, she wipes the tears from her face, her feet prance under the desk, she opens a new mail. Fingers peck at the keys. Tanja is in a spiral of conflict.

© The Author(s), under exclusive license to Springer Fachmedien Wiesbaden GmbH, part of Springer Nature 2022
A. Hartmann-Piraudeau, *Out of the spiral of conflict*,
https://doi.org/10.1007/978-3-658-39779-1_1

Nina, Martin and Tanja are in a spiral of conflict and so are many people. They are in private conflicts, argue at work or are at odds with themselves. Organisations, parties and countries are also affected – they get caught up in the whirlpool of their conflicts.

What dynamics do conflicts take on and how do they develop? What happens to us when we enter the conflict spiral. How does our thinking, our view on things and our interests change? What does the conflict do to us and how do we get out of the vortex? That is what this book is about.

It is based on scientific findings from psychology and conflict research. In order to make the behaviours vivid, I will report anonymously from real cases from my practice. I am a mediator and expert for conflicts and have been observing for years how people and organizations deal with conflicts and how they manage in most cases to leave their conflict spirals.

Psychology has known for a long time that we are not rational beings. We do not act soberly and objectively. Our behavior is influenced by many factors, feelings play a role, but also psychological mechanisms and patterns that we are not aware of. The deeper we are in a conflict, the more "others" take over. The "others" are our inner voices, our physical reactions, changed feelings and also protective functions of our brain that are now in charge. The conflict has us-no longer are we controlling, but we are being controlled. Understanding who is steering us and how to reclaim the steering wheel helps us clarify conflict. Our own and those of others.

The first part is about understanding the *nature* of conflict.

- What is conflict anyway?
- What are the conflicts?
- Where do they occur?
- What are their dynamics?

That's the basis.

- What influence does our behaviour have?
- What differences in conflict management do different personality types exhibit?
- What are the conflict resolution strategies?

This is described in the second part.

The third part is about the conflict spiral and conflict resolution:

- What happens to us when we have conflict?
- How do we act in conflict?
- And how do we get out of the spiral again?

2

The Nature of Conflicts

What is it that we actually call conflict? Many conflict researchers have developed definitions and described conflicts. I will pick out a few selected ones later. First, however, I would like to take you to the desert. We are not alone, Jim Button and Lukas the Locomotive Driver have already arrived there. The two heroes from Michael Ende's well-known novel travel through unknown worlds in a locomotive. One way leads them to the desert 'to the end of the world'. As they travel along, a giant suddenly appears on the horizon. The two are terribly frightened. Jim Knopf and Lukas the Engine Driver run for their lives. In the other direction, away from the giant who scares them. After some time they stop, out of breath they dare a look over their shoulder. But to their great fright, the giant has not grown smaller on the horizon, but much larger. They retreat, fear filled, look the giant in the face and run backwards. As they do so, they see that the further away they get, the bigger the giant becomes. Little Jim Knopf is beside himself with fear, the experienced Luke finally stops and thinks. Fleeing doesn't seem to work. Bravely they raise their eyes and look the giant cautiously in the eye. He doesn't actually look that scary. Is he smiling? Luke takes heart and waves his white handkerchief as a sign of his peaceful intent and in the hope that the giant will share it. Slowly, the giant approaches – walking with big strides right towards them. What happens next is like a miracle: the closer they get to each other, the smaller the giant becomes. As he stands close to them, they meet an old, friendly gentleman named Tur-Tur. Mr. Tur-Tur tells them his story and they become friends. Mr. Tur-Tur is an *illusory giant*.[1]

---

[1] Loosely based on Ende, Michael: Jim Knopf und Lukas der Lokomotivführer. 1999.

© The Author(s), under exclusive license to Springer Fachmedien Wiesbaden GmbH, part of Springer Nature 2022
A. Hartmann-Piraudeau, *Out of the spiral of conflict*,
https://doi.org/10.1007/978-3-658-39779-1_2

Conflicts are often also: *illusory giants*. Most of the time they appear suddenly or completely unexpectedly. They pile up in front of us like mountains. We get scared, we feel uncomfortable and do what we intuitively do in such situations to protect ourselves: we flee. As we flee, however, we find that the conflicts don't get smaller. Most of the time, they get bigger. We feel like they are chasing us. We can't shake them, they shadow our lives. Not until we look them in the face. When we confront them, they become comprehensible to us. We recognize their nature, we may understand where they come from. When we deal with them and have the possibility to make peace with them, they often become important life companions for us. We learn from conflicts we have overcome. New paths open up, which we would not have seen before.

> If you take some time and think for a moment about your last pacified conflict. Do you see what positive sides this conflict had?

From a neutral point of view, conflicts mean development. If there were no conflicts, there would be no development. Not in us and not in society. However, there are constructive, "healthy" ways and destructive, difficult paths of conflict resolution. In order to understand this, I will go into more detail about different types of conflict in the next chapter.

2.1 Constructive Conflicts

Without conflict there would be no development. At first, this sounds strange to our ears. To understand this idea, it helps to take a sober look at conflicts. A conflict arises from a clash of interests. Two people, two teams, several countries, different organizations have different needs that are expressed in interests. These different interests are usually negotiated between the parties involved. This happens in our everyday life in many small moments and on the political stage of world affairs, for example, in large negotiation processes that last for years.

> **Example**
>
> *Johanna and her husband want to go out for dinner. Johanna loves light meals, her husband Marc likes hearty food. The "vegetablegarden" restaurant around the corner offers cuisine that is just to Johanna's taste. The big Bone fetten Ochsen at the end of the street is her husband's favourite restaurant. They have different needs. Even though they won't argue and will have a nice evening together at the restaurant at the end of the evening, this is a conflict. The two of them are negotiating their interests. They may go out to eat here today and there soon, they may prefer to cook something for themselves, they may order from both restaurants, or they may do something completely different. Neither will feel oppressive at the end of the evening. The conflict has led to a solution in which, in the best case, both interests have been taken into account – an everyday negotiation process in which two different interests lead to a common, new solution.*

In science, conflicts are important innovators. Different ideas and opinions on a topic inspire the depth of the discussion. If there were no different interests, i.e. if everyone always agreed and had no opposing opinions, then it would be convenient to stick with the first (thought) model. A company's development department is well advised to encourage conflict.

If we think of conflicts of interest in society, then these are, for example, employer/employee conflicts, conflicts over equality or conflicts between generations. These areas are associated with intensive negotiation processes. Thanks to many conflicts that reflect differences of interest, our society is constantly evolving. The current climate debate is also characterised by different interests and representatives of these interests. Finding solutions to such global differences of interest is complicated and protracted. This complexity, which arises from numerous different interests, is at the same time the source of solutions. Different opinions form the basis for dialogue processes to take place at all and for the future to be shaped.

In science, these conflicts are called functional or productive. They serve a purpose, they are necessary preconditions for change, renewal, reform and progress. Productive describes the quality that something new emerges through conflict.

Most people find this positive view of conflict difficult. We usually associate negative feelings with conflicts. Understanding conflicts as productive, leading to something new, as drivers of innovation, requires a change of perspective. In my mediation practice I work with people who want to clarify their conflicts. At the end of each clarification, I ask the participants what their conflict has shown them. What positive insights or paths the conflict has opened up for them.

I was touched by one client's response:

> **Example**
>
> *It was a conflict of inheritance. Two sisters couldn't manage to divide their parents' inheritance without arguing. The money wasn't the problem. It was about the parental home, memory pieces and a dog. In mediation, it soon became apparent that the conflict over the items and the dog, were proxies for deeper conflicts about recognition, appreciation, justice and roles in the family. The two sisters had not been in contact with each other for ten years, the arguments leading up to the mediation were heated and both felt hurt by the other. Accordingly, it was difficult for both of them to get back into conversation with each other in this situation. In the mediation they managed to open up and talk about these deep issues with each other. The house, the dog, and the mementos became side issues. There was a lot of crying. First alone, then together. Eventually the sisters were able to look each other in the eye. In the course of the mediation they understood each other better, even comforted each other, and in the process very gently reknotted the rope of sibling connection. At the end, I asked them what was good about this conflict over their parents' inheritance, which had caused them both months of sleepless nights, pain and tears. After quite a while of silence, one sister said, "I found my sister back and that is a great gift to me." The other could not speak for tears of emotion and came around the table, calling the sister by her childhood pet name and hugging her.*

It doesn't always have to be so essential, sometimes it's hard for us to see what was good about the conflict. It is insights about ourselves that we take away: How we want to handle situations in the future? Where our boundaries lie? What we really value? Or what happens to us when we are in conflict?

However, even if we have experienced that a conflict has brought something good in our lives, we do not look forward to new conflicts. We usually perceive conflicts as stressful. When the conflict giant appears in front of us, we prefer to run away.

2.2 Destructive/Dysfunctional Conflicts

The conflict emerges and we flee. This is a typical first reaction, which makes sense. Avoidance is a possible solution strategy. How appropriate or inappropriate it is for the current conflict case has to be evaluated in the situation. If we think of our ancestors, there was an everyday conflict there. In search of something edible, comes a wild animal. The tiger usually has a simple need: hunger. Man in this situation also has an obvious interest: Survival. Running away was a good alternative in this case. Annihilation is also on the list of conflict resolution methods. A few hundred years later, people in this situation no longer trusted their sprinting skills, but used modern technology and shot the wild animal. This is an example that is not morally complicated. However, there are other, less clear constellations.

The vast majority of destructive, dysfunctional conflicts hurt. They can be small temporary disturbances of our well-being, but they can develop into manifest psychosomatic symptoms. Neurologists have found that in situations of social discomfort – caused by conflict or exclusion, for example – the same pain-processing areas in the brain are targeted that are active when one experiences physical pain. The result is a "conflict pain".

People who are in emotional and upsetting conflicts report various complaints: e.g. insomnia, headaches, lack of concentration, dejection, confusion, increased relapses of existing chronic diseases.

But at what point is a conflict no longer helpful and welcome, but stressful? Many conflict researchers have dealt with this in their definition of conflicts. In agreement, a conflict is described as a difference of interests in which at least **one person** feels impaired and the respective preferred **options for action are** not or do not **appear to be realisable at the same time.**

At this point, let us think again of our ancestors and the wild animal. The human feels impaired in the situation, since he cannot continue to pursue his plan (the search for food) and becomes afraid. The preferred course of action of this human would be to get food undisturbed and unmolested, but since the preferred course of action of the wild animal is to fill its stomach, these do not seem to be feasible at the same time.

The term conflict comes from the Latin "conflictus" and means collision. This clash mainly concerns the level of interests and needs. A conflict can be seen as a social interaction between individuals, groups or even organizations. It is interesting to note that already when a person feels affected, there is a conflict.

I often observe this constellation in team conflicts: One person no longer feels comfortable in the professional team. Feels excluded by other colleagues, is of the opinion that his interests are no longer heard and withdraws. This person feels a conflict.

> **Example**
>
> This is what happened in Mr. Meier's team: Mr. Meier is the team leader of an IT team. Mr. Thoma is the employee who suffers because he feels excluded. Mr. Thoma is in conflict. And he has been for quite some time. After some effort, he has approached his team leader, Mr. Meier, and explained how he feels and that the situation is getting to him. The team consists of four other colleagues. Mr. Meier, as the manager, sees it as his job to resolve this conflict. Therefore he talks to the three other colleagues. All three colleagues react with surprise and assure him that they have no problem with Mr. Thoma and no conflict. Mr. Meier is happy about this "good news" and immediately shares it with Mr. Thoma. The next day Mr Thoma is ill. When he comes back to the office after a long absence, he seems unsettled and sensitive. He is absent more often than before. He does his work more slowly and his depressed mood radiates to his colleagues. Mr. Meier fears losing Mr. Thoma as a valuable expert. He contacts me with the question: is there such a thing, a conflict that only one person feels?

Yes, there is and this is an important part of the definition and understanding of conflict. We remember once again: **if someone feels that their thinking, feeling or wanting is being impaired, then there is a conflict.** If there is a conflict, then it is also worthwhile to work on and solve it before it escalates. Especially if the constellation is such that the persons or groups in a collision of interests depend on each other, cannot get out of each other's way or are under pressure to reach an agreement. This can be assumed for work teams as well as for most family constellations. Running away is not a good option here, because conflicts develop their own dynamics, which you will learn more about later.

Back to Mr. Meier and his team:

> **Example**
>
> Mr Meier, as he himself later reflected, was happy when he learned from Mr Thoma's three colleagues that they had no conflict. His conclusion was: so everything is good after all. He was relieved not to have to deal with these "emotional" issues any further and was of the firm opinion that Mr Thoma was also changed and calmed by this news, his feelings. For Mr. Thoma, however, this analysis by his supervisor was devastating: his sense of exclusion intensified. He questioned his perceptions, his mental carousel sped up, he could no longer concentrate, he became insecure towards his colleagues, who acted as if nothing had happened, and he felt shame towards his boss, who might think he was trying to cause trouble. Things deteriorated, he became ill and considered quitting several times. When Mr. Meier and his team decided to mediate, several things became clear. The three colleagues felt very strongly that something had been wrong for some time. However, they too wanted to avoid the debate. And the three are different types than Mr. Thoma, who worries a lot about social contacts and is prone to self-doubt. In the open discussion, the actual conflict (it was about the division of work and the assumption of responsibility) could be clarified and also the fact that it was not just one person who felt the conflict after all.

Even dysfunctional conflicts can be transformed into constructive conflicts through clarification. The fact, however, that they are often connected with injuries and pain on the way there and take up a lot of space in our thinking and feeling in the acute state, turns them into horror giants.

2.3 Hot and Cold Conflicts

There is another classification of conflicts, which also lie on two poles: The temperature of conflicts. To speak of the temperature of conflicts may sound strange at first glance. However, this categorization is actually used in this way in conflict research and has proven to be very descriptive. One of the aims of this categorisation is to describe the quality of conflicts more precisely in order to draw conclusions about the best possible method of resolution.

'Hot conflicts', that is almost self-speaking. These are conflicts that are usually acute. "Tempers are running high", "the atmosphere is tense", "it feels like it is about to explode", "I am about to burst", "my patience is wearing thin" ... These are typical descriptions from and about people who are in hot conflicts. There is screaming, crying, we see red faces. Anger and rage play a role but also despair, sadness and hurt can be emotions of a hot conflict. When we come into a room where people are arguing, we sense when the atmosphere is heated, tense and aggressive. It is then probably, a hot conflict. When we talk to people about their conflicts and they get emotional, angry and agitated, then it is most likely a hot conflict as well.

In stark contrast, the cold conflict:

> **Example**
>
> *We come into a room, here the employees of a branch of a bank are working. The atmosphere is quiet. No one is talking to each other. The monitors, coffee cups, scattered flower pots and folders form small fortresses around everyone's workstation. A concentrated working atmosphere, you might think. A customer arrives, no one stands up. After a few minutes, Mrs. Sanders moans to herself, "Always me," and walks sullenly to the customer counter. "Yes, always you," Mr. Stiel hisses from another corner. Mrs Jahn rolls her eyes. After that, silence reigns again. At 4:00 p.m. Mr. Stiel packs his bag mumbles something like "Bye" and leaves the room without further comment, soon followed by the other two.*

As observers, we feel it is not a concentrated working atmosphere, but an extraordinary coldness. Gram, cynicism, being offended, withdrawal, resentment, such qualities have the feelings in a cold conflict. There is little to no talking to each other, body and eye contact is avoided, facial expressions are frozen, there is little laughter and certainly none together. What happened here in the branch of the bank of a small town and in other cold conflicts?

Often they have developed from hot conflicts. At some point there was an occasion that upset one or more of the parties involved. From this disgruntlement a hardening arose. That hardening turned into a dispute. A spiral of conflict, which we will learn more about later, was set in motion. In the beginning, everyone involved was very upset, discussing it out loud, talking about the conflict at home, and dreaming about it. However, this conflict was never resolved. In the case of the bank, its origins go back ten years.

Experience has shown that hot conflicts are easier to resolve for those involved. The disputants are still close to their emotions at this moment. They can usually express what they are feeling. They can remember when and where the conflict began, and they have an acute emotional charge that most people wish they could get rid of. The cold conflicts are thick icebergs. Over the years, the original issues have become covered with many layers of other sensitivities. The core lies far below, often buried and often difficult for those involved to reach. During a clarification, in most cases there are major differences in the conflict histories in these conflicts. The parties then accuse each other of telling the untruth. But that is not the point: the stories, for example how the conflict started and at which points it became particularly stressful, are experienced and stored differently by people. Everyone has a different perception about what happened and renders it differently accordingly. We call this *constructivism*. It refers to the fact that we construct our reality ourselves.

> Think of a house in a garden! Paint this house in your mind.

If I were to ask you now to send me your association of a house in a garden and I were to lay all the paintings of all the readers next to each other, a colourful city would emerge. With big wild parks and little crooked witch houses next to fir trees, from skyscrapers with a front garden to mountain huts next to bare rocks. They have constructed their image and none of the images is more right or wrong than another. So it is with reflections on a conflict. Each of the parties has a different view of it. This different view is not, as is often accused in heated discussions, a distortion of the facts, a lie or even a perceptual disorder. No, it is human and related to our individual experience and perception. This perception is influenced, among other things, by our socialization, by our experiences or by our world view that has developed in the course of our lives.

Back to the cold conflicts, especially in these it is difficult for the disputants to get to their own source of the conflict. Why did the argument start then? What hit me? What feelings did I have and how have they changed over time?

In order to clarify the conflict, it is necessary to get to these deeper layers, to the starting point of the conflict. With icebergs you have to drill deeper. In conflict resolution, this often means that clarifications take longer and that layers of ice have to be broken open to one's own openness, to wanting to get into contact with the other person at all.

Even though hot conflicts are easier to resolve, they are often not resolved. Over time they become cold conflicts. There are different reasons why people then decide to resolve a conflict after many years. In the case of the bank employee, it was because more and more customer complaints *were* coming to the team leader: *"The employees were getting grumpier and grumpier, the mood was so bad."*

It was only the threat of losing customers that prompted the team to start a conflict resolution process.

Why many hot conflicts are not resolved is understandable. The atmosphere of hot conflicts, makes us afraid. Moreover, especially in the workplace, we often have the good hope that 'things will calm down'. Rarely does that work, often it doesn't. More on this later, in the dynamics of conflict.

Example

I remember Mr. Jansen, project manager of a team of experts in the chemical industry. Mr. Jansen called me, he was very irritated. That morning he was chairing a team meeting of his team of experts on what he called a very important and time-critical project. In the meeting, the mood exploded for him, completely unexpectedly. Two of the experts shouted at each other, a third interfered and two others left the room without a word. Mr. Jansen tried to bring calm into the meeting, but was unable to calm the disputants. He saw no other option than to break off the meeting and leave the room himself. The two disputants left shortly after him. Back in his office, Mr. Jansen was,, very irritated and, angry that the situation had escalated so much, and unhappy with himself for failing to cool down the dispute. He tells me that this was not a spontaneous conflict, but that the outburst felt like a barrel that had overflowed. Mr. Jansen sat down at the computer shortly after the meeting to send an invitation to colleagues, for the continuation of the conversation. When I asked if he had addressed this particular situation in which the meeting had broken up, he immediately replied: Of course! He had written in the mail to the colleagues that there would be a next meeting on this topic, since today's meeting was not productive for known reasons, and he would like to use this way to tell the colleagues that he expected that at the next meeting the discussion would be on the factual level and emotional outbursts and conflicts like today would please be avoided. He wanted to know from me whether his approach was okay and whether I had a tip for him on how he could keep these conflicts out of the meetings if they should arise again.

For Mr. Jansen, this situation was personally difficult. He is a calm analytical type, and rather a conflict avoider. The conflict made him feel very uncomfortable and his reaction was to 'run away'. He retreated to his office and communicated by email, a medium that due to the lack of direct feedback from the other person, is popular in difficult communication situations. His messages were: 'The meeting was not productive. We need to keep working. Please remain objective!

He would prefer not to hear anything more about the conflict. Mr. Jansen is a smart and reflective man and already while we were talking on the phone it occurred to him that it might not be a good strategy to 'sweep the conflict under the carpet'. I reinforced this reflection to him and told him about hot and cold conflict. Since Mr. Jansen had observed from the beginning that this was not a spontaneous tantrum of a colleague who would calm down after sleeping on it for a night, but that a barrel has come to overflowing here, it is high time to openly address this conflict. If this does not happen here, there is a great danger that the conflict will freeze and with it the dynamics and efficiency of his team. Mr. Jansen has changed his invitation to the next meeting. He managed to talk about the conflict with his team and gave the participants the space to present their perspectives. After initial uncertainty, the conversation was accepted very openly and gratefully by his colleagues. Since then, Mr. Jansen has been holding regular team talks about cooperation and is gradually learning to actively confront the conflict giant.

2.4 The Escalation of Conflicts

When we talk about the escalation of conflicts, it helps to imagine once again Mr. Tur-Tur the illusory giant. The further the viewers run away from him, the bigger and more threatening he becomes.

Conflicts have the dynamic to escalate. Friedrich Glasl, a well-known conflict researcher from Austria, has studied this phenomenon for many years. He classifies escalating conflicts on the basis of "conflict stages"[2]. At each stage the conflict gets worse. Whereas at the beginning of an emerging disagreement, discussions among each other help to resolve it, this becomes less likely the further the conflict descends the stairs. The special thing about escalating conflicts is the phenomenon that, over time, the parties involved in the conflict lose sight of their actual goals and their own interests. At some point, the parties involved are primarily concerned with harming the others rather than pursuing their own original interests. This classification of the degree of escalation of conflicts according to Glasl reads a little like a detective story:

It begins harmlessly: Initial tensions arise with the occasional clash of differing opinions. At this point, the participants do not yet perceive their interaction as a conflict. They are everyday differences of interest that can dissolve again. However, when this harmless conflict hardens, opinions become more fundamental. Arguments are brought forth more emotionally and the mood of those involved is noticeably dampened. The conflict may have deeper causes.

At the next stage, the conflicting parties consider strategies to convince the other of their arguments. The harmless disagreement from before now leads to an argument. One wants to put the other under pressure. In one's own perception, a black and white picture emerges. One's own conviction grows that what one thinks is right. The arguments of the other one are always frequently judged as incorrect and wrong. Debates arise that are increasingly polemical.

Then actions follow instead of words. The disputants increase the pressure on the other to assert themselves or their own opinion. For example, conversations are broken off, the tone becomes louder. The atmosphere and encounters, even outside the conflict discussions, become cooler. Avoidance is one strategy, attack and aggression another. In this phase there is often little verbal communication. The conflict quickly intensifies. Compassion for the other person is lost and we see ourselves more and more in the role of the good guy, while we accuse the other person of bad intentions.

---

[2] Glasl, F. (1992), Conflict management: a handbook for the diagnosis and treatment of conflicts for organizations and their consultants. third edition, Stuttgart: Verlag Freies Geistesleben. S. 218 f.

There is still a way back to this point. If the conflict is resolved now, the chances of finding a solution for both parties are good. If the disputants do not continue to run away at this point, but pull out the white handkerchief, they can manage to resolve their conflict on their own. If they flee, then the conflict giant becomes so powerful that it becomes increasingly difficult to turn around and make peace further down the road without outside help:

The conflict intensifies. The conflict parties look for sympathizers for their own cause. Thus, conflicts often spread further in family, friends or even work circles. Coalitions and thus conflict fronts develop. Everyone believes to be in the right. Often the conflict partner is denounced. At this point it is no longer about the actual matter, but about winning the conflict so that the opponent loses. One's own interests, which were still very important at the very beginning, move into the background. The focus is on preserving one's own image and looking better than the other.

At the next level of escalation, insinuations become popular weapons. The opponent is to be destroyed in his identity. There is no longer any trust between the disputants. The parties try to destroy the moral credibility of the other. The other should "lose face". For this purpose, different registers are pulled out. For example, stories are told about the other person that show him or her in a bad light; third parties are put under pressure to also reveal negative sides or actions of the other person to others, if possible. In this phase, people often act imaginatively. The experiences lose their chronological order. New stories emerge about how the dispute began and what relationship the two disputants used to have with each other. This phase has a threatening effect on the conflict partners. Even manipulations are not shied away from, if they serve to make the partner appear in a bad light. The parties involved are afraid of losing face and rise to a higher level of escalation:

Threats are now used to try to control the situation. Threats illustrate one's own power. Often a threat is made with a demand (this will cost you 50,000 €), with an action (I will sue you) or with a sanction (then I will leave the company). Threats are backed up by showing the potential for enforcement: a letter from a lawyer, an application for a new job. Here, proportions determine the credibility of the threat.

By this point, the outer and inner mood has darkened. It is no longer about finding a good solution for both, but that the other loses this "fight". If conflicts have escalated to this point, they can no longer be resolved by the conflict participants themselves. Now conflict resolution methods from outside are needed: mediation can be one, clarification assistance, moderation or even court proceedings or therapies. The context determines the most suitable method. But we have not yet reached the bottom of the escalation cellar.

THE NINE ESCALATION LEVELS ACCORDING TO F. GLASL

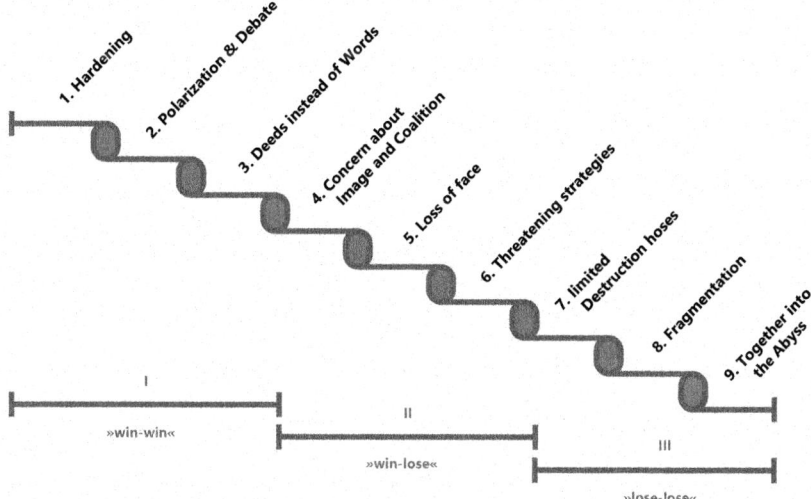

Fig. 2.1 The escalation stages freely adapted from Friedrich Glasl

It continues with the limited destruction. Thereby the opponent is to be harmed with all tricks. The opponent is no longer perceived as a sentient human being, since one's own feelings and moral ideas about dealing with others are lost in this phase. From here on, a limited own damage is accepted and already seen as a gain, should the damage of the opponent be greater than the own. In this phase (previously unknown) criminal energies often appear. Participants are in a tunnel, they lose the ability to evaluate their own actions.

It's going downhill. The next stage is to destroy the enemy's support system. The impacts become larger. Those who are close to the conflict partner also become enemies. The conflict is actively expanded and continued with people from the environment of the conflict partner.

Glasl calls the last stage "together into the abyss". One calculates one's own destruction in order to defeat the opponent. We have arrived at war. Unfortunately, a white handkerchief no longer helps here. Even the help of a neutral dispute mediator is no longer effective here. Conflicts of this level can only be defused by external power interventions. It is obvious: There are no winners. Both parties to the conflict will have lost in the end (Fig. 2.1).

When we (neutral) mediators encounter a conflict in practice, it is helpful to make a rough classification for the choice of the mediation method. It is considered on which stage the conflict has already reached.

People in conflict situations are in a state of emergency. Sides come to light or actions are taken that one would never have thought one was capable of in peaceful times. If conflict resolution succeeds, it is not infrequently associated with the recognition of one's own dark side. I remember a conflict between two foremen of a mechanical engineering company.

> **Example**
>
> *The two have spiraled into conflict over initially small arguments and competitive thoughts. This conflict has escalated: Colleagues on each shift were dragged into it, and personal and sometimes intimate stories were circulated to each other. A sad climax to the conflict was an unflattering photo that Mr. Lose had snapped of Mr. Brown while changing clothes, unnoticed by Mr. Brown, and sent it to others. For Mr. Brown, this photo was a loss of face. He felt ashamed and went on the counterattack. Mr. Lose should also be exposed and preferably in front of his boss and all his colleagues. Mr. Brown stayed late at the company one evening and tampered with a milling machine that was Mr. Lose's responsibility the next morning. The idea was to break as many parts as possible without being noticed. That would drive up the scrap balance for that shift and pretty much guarantee a lot of trouble with the supervisor. The employee who operated the machine quickly noticed that something was wrong. Mr. Lose called in sick that day and the employee informed the team leader. The team leader also learned this way that Mr. Lose's team, believed only one person could be behind this manipulation: Mr. Brown and his team. The team leader realized the seriousness of the situation. Up until now, he wanted to hear little of the argument because, "we're not in kindergarten here, we're at work, so get a grip!" But enough was enough now. Fortunately, nothing had happened, but if the staff's suspicions were correct, things couldn't go on like this. There was brief internal discussion about whether the police should be called in for deliberately tampering with the machine. But that was rejected. They didn't want to bring any more unrest into the team. The team leader suggested mediation to the two disputants. In a joint conversation, both admitted their actions to each other. They will never become friends, but they found a way to deal and work with each other respectfully. The turning point in this conflict resolution happened at that point when both managed to distance themselves a bit and look from the outside at what had happened between them over the last two years. Both were affected and shocked by what dark sides of their personalities had come to light in this dispute. Both men, who described themselves as "hard shell soft core" types, managed to understand how each other must have felt. The key to clarification, however, lay in self-knowledge: "I don't want to be such a monster and never want to become one again," said one of them at the end, they shook hands.*

2.5 The Aura of Conflict

By the aura of conflicts is meant here the radiation, in the sense of expansion and spread of conflicts. As already described, when conflicts come to a head, coalitions are sought quite early on. From this moment on, the conflict does not only affect the disputants exclusively, but also the environment. It is a natural need in times of uncertainty to seek support. It gives us security when others share our opinion. In the context of conflict, this means convincing others that our stance is the right one and the other person's is not. People in conflict put a lot of energy and resources into this coalition building. Close confidants such as the wife or husband, the best friend, the parents the favourite colleague become involved in the dispute quite early. They are thus indirectly affected by the conflict as they are also unable to assert their interests towards the husband, wife, girlfriend etc. as usual and are more or less burdened by this conflict because they are worried for example. We have often experienced scenes like this in our lives.

> **Example**
>
> *The Haas family is sitting down to dinner. Mrs. Haas seems thoughtful and absent. This has been going on for a few days. When asked what was going on, Mrs Haas tells them about the argument with her colleague. This is not the first time the family has heard about this colleague. Mrs Haas has been angry with this woman several times before. But now Mr. Haas has had enough: "The whole atmosphere is destroyed because of this strange colleague. What kind of a demanding person must she be that she manages to wear down even my usually cheerful wife like this?" Mrs. Haas tells what happened from her point of view. At this point, the conflict is already more than a mere clash of interests. Mrs. Haas sees the right action in herself and the mistakes in her colleague and reports to her family accordingly. Of course, she expects loyalty and backing from the family. And she gets it. When questioned critically about her own actions in this dispute, she reacts impatiently and indignantly. At this point she is no longer prepared to develop understanding for her colleague or to reflect critically on her own actions. The family supports her in order not to get into a conflict of her own on the one hand and on the other hand to show the loyalty that Mrs. Haas expects from her closest environment. They support Mrs. Haas, among other things, in the hope and their own interest that this support will finally lead to a better mood at dinner in the evening. The first coalition is formed and this circle of allies, the family, is regularly informed about the updates of the conflict story.*

Soon people in this close circle experience their own emotions against the conflict partner (in this case Mrs. Haas' colleagues), although they may not even know him personally. This close circle is also used by people in conflicts to express themselves, to cry, to unload ballast. The more a conflict expands, the more often it dominates conversations. The closest circle becomes conflict participants. The attempt to get the best friend out of this spiral, "can we talk about something else for once" or even "I can also understand your colleague", is usually judged by those involved in the conflict as a breach of trust and loyalty and is not infrequently answered with a break-off of contact and a new, further conflict. Such "new" conflict ramifications are often found in long-lasting family conflicts. For example, when two adult siblings get into an argument and new conflict fronts are opened up by the coalitions formed and the efforts of some family members to mediate the dispute. Suddenly, not only the two siblings quarrel, but also a conflict arises between uncles and aunts.

The aura of conflict often extends far beyond the closest circle. Not only emotional coalitions, like those in the family, but strategic coalitions are formed:

> **Example**
>
> In the case of Mrs Haas and her colleague, it is the other colleagues. A real race for new alliances begins here. A total of twelve other colleagues work in Ms Haas' department. They have long sensed that the air between Ms Haas and her colleague is thick. It didn't take long for both colleagues to talk about the dispute on different occasions. Ms Haas has not spoken to all her colleagues but she has spoken to the five closest to her. At lunch, at the coffee machine, on the way home together, Ms. Haas complained to them about their mutual colleague. Some colleagues were happy to listen to this, as they find this particular colleague to be looking for a fight anyway. Other colleagues felt uncomfortable when Ms Haas told you about the conflict. They didn't want to get involved, they also get along well with the other colleague and "don't want to get involved". But when you said this more or less directly to Ms Haas, she reacted in a distant way. She spoke less than usual and turned away. Soon the colleagues began to feel uncomfortable themselves. Two of the hesitant colleagues sought to speak with Ms. Haas and when she complained to them one more time, they failed to maintain their neutrality and agreed with Ms. Haas. Mrs. Haas encouraged this and again became more friendly in her dealings with them. Little by little the coalitions between Mrs. Haas and her colleague grew and strengthened, until the whole circle of colleagues stood more or less openly to one side or the other. Only very occasionally were female colleagues able to stay out of the conflict. They became outsiders to the whole department. Over time, new lines of conflict were added between the two office fronts. In order to show that they belonged to the Haas coalition, the tone became harsher when the coalition of female colleagues made a contribution. Distrust arose when new tasks were assigned, and conversations with the boss were eyed suspiciously. After four months, the department was in a state of emergency. Productivity dropped. Sick leave increased. The mood was bad. An escalated conflict had manifested itself and hardly anyone involved could really name how it came about.

This course of conflict in the work environment is typical. Depending on the constellation and the types of people involved, more or less people in the circle of colleagues become parties to the conflict. The fact that the conflict spreads from two disputants to the environment is pre-programmed. Either directly, as in this case, in which the colleagues ended up being just as affected by the conflict as Ms. Haas and her colleague were in the beginning, or indirectly: the colleagues suffer from the bad mood, the irritation, the sadness of the disputants. Team activities lose their light, carefree tone, the sensitivities of the two disputants have to be taken into account again and again in order to avoid an explosion. Staying motivated in such an environment requires active counter-management.

Various studies[3] have calculated conflict costs in the workplace. They come to considerable losses due to decreasing efficiency, increased absenteeism and dismissals resulting from conflicts.

Managers have a special role to play in this situation. They are there to organize the work efficiently. The responsibility of managers for the quality of cooperation is an important factor here. This involves aspects such as respectful communication, clear information, appreciative behavior or trusting interaction. This is often referred to as the "culture" of a department or team. Since conflicts do not calm themselves down, but escalate, develop an aura, demotivate entire teams and consequently lead to poorer working conditions and results, dealing with conflicts in the team is a crucial task of every manager.

But what does "working on" mean? If a manager has not yet dealt with conflicts, their clarification and dynamics, then they often react like any other "conflict layman". The conflict giant shows up and they turn and run. The arguments for this behaviour in the work context are e.g. the following: *"We have to take care of the essential tasks, we don't have time for such spirits"; "We are not in kindergarten here, everyone should solve their own conflicts"; "I am an engineer and not a psychologist, please stay objective!"*.

Running away seems to work well at first, because the employees usually strive to display a desired behavior towards the manager. If they sense that the conflict is causing displeasure with the manager, they first consciously try to keep it away from the manager. As a rule, however, this does not work for too long. This is because the conflict continues to run its course at their own hierarchical level. At some point, either the pressure of suffering increases for those involved in the conflict, or the conflict becomes too colorful for the group of colleagues. In both cases, the path leads back to the manager. At this point, many managers intuitively feel that "running away won't help

---

[3] S. et al. Conflict Cost Study. The costs of frictional losses in industrial companies. KPMG 2009.

anymore". Now the first talks are held with the two disputants. At this point it regularly happens that the manager unwittingly takes on the role of judge. In order to get the conflict off the table as quickly as possible, a widespread strategy of managers is to listen to the positions of both parties in order to form their own opinion and decide who is right and who is wrong, in order to be able to continue working undisturbed as quickly as possible afterwards. This strategy is familiar to us. In the course of our socialization we have experienced it again and again. When parents settled a dispute between siblings and became detectives to find out who really ate the last cookie. The memories of most school conflicts are similar, too. When two argue, it's not uncommon for the teacher to end up deciding right from wrong and handing out one-sided punishments to support that perspective.

With the exception of the judicial process, where the administration of justice is based on general conventions and laws, the search for 'right' and 'wrong', for the 'truth' of the conflict, is a dangerous dead end.

Soon the manager senses during the individual discussions with those involved in the conflict that everyone has their own conflict story. Whether or not Ms. Mueller actually went home ten minutes early on Tuesday evening two weeks ago and switched off the printer so that others in the office could no longer print from that point on and this led to a delay in the project delivery will be difficult to comprehend in retrospect. As a conflict clarifier (in this role is the manager), it is not expedient to get bogged down in the search for this truth. It is better to understand the individual conflict perceptions of each party and try to bring them back into conversation with each other. In the effort to 'understand someone', however, lies a difficulty. Again, back to the situation:

The manager has invited the two parties to the conflict to talk. What the manager may not reflect is that the two disputants are looking for a coalition. In the coalition search there are important and less important coalition partners. The executive is important, even very important. In the conversation, both disputants will sometimes more sometimes less strategically, sometimes more sometimes less consciously try to convince the executive that their position is the right one and the other's is the wrong one. The disputants both come with the deepest conviction that they are doing right and the other is wrong. They often do not shy away from exaggerating what has happened to support their position. In doing so, they closely observe how the interlocutor, in this case their manager, reacts. An approving and well-intentioned *"I can understand you"* or *"That's really mean how you're being treated"* or *"That's just not right"*, are quickly interpreted as approval and positive signals with regard to the sought-after coalition. However, since both disputants have 'experienced' injustice and wrongdoing, both are 'understood' by the leader. The interpretation of what is said becomes a certainty that the leader is on their side. This encourages the disputants to escalate the dispute further. The manager, who simply wanted to express understanding for both of them, quickly becomes part of the conflict. If the manager also takes on the role of judge in this conflict and says who he thinks is right or wrong, the displeasure is pre-programmed. As a rule, one party is dissatisfied with a "judge's decision". Often both feel patronized and react with a loss of trust.

But how can the manager act if he or she is responsible for conflict management? In the vast majority of cases of conflict in the workplace, neutral moderation by the manager as an aid to self-determined resolution of the conflict is a good way forward. In doing so, they try to help in a neutral role to leave the conflict spiral. You can read more about this in Chap. 5.

If you've gotten this far, you've learned the essential dynamics of conflict.

The next chapter is about all of us and how we argue. Us humans with our imprints, attitudes, patterns and individual characteristics. With so much difference between us, it is no wonder that it bangs, right?

3

Conflict Types

Maybe you recognize yourself in the examples you read here, maybe you are surprised why people say or do something like this and think to yourself that you would have acted very differently in this situation. This is what complicates looking at conflicts, their escalation and assessment- there is no one set pattern of events and equally no one resolution strategy for all conflicts and that is up to us- the actors, the disputants. When we get into a conflict, we quickly slip into a pattern of looking critically at the others and making sweeping judgements about their behaviour. I often hear statements like: *"My boss has no empathy, there's no point in explaining my situation to him"* or *"you can't argue with my husband, he explodes immediately"* or *"my girlfriend is always in a huff and then there's no point in arguing."*

Through our genetic makeup, our experiences, our bodies, our knowledge, our observations, and our relationships, we have become personalities of our own. Others, no matter how close they are to us, are different.

In conflict it is advisable not to forget this simple truth and not to focus too much on the faults and shortcomings of our disputants, but to reflect on ourselves.

Our behavior and the subsequent behavior of others is not disconnected, but mutually dependent. This is called **reciprocity.** The word comes from sociology and means reciprocity and mutuality. It is the basic principle of human action.

> **Example**
>
> *If I look at a friendly face, I am more likely to look back with a smile than if angry eyes look at me. If I do someone a favor, it is likely that they will return the favor later.*

Our behaviour influences the behaviour of our counterpart. In a conflict, it is therefore advisable to start with oneself and reflect on how I am behaving at the moment, why I am doing, saying or not doing something and what effect this might have on my counterpart.

There is another argument for starting with introspection in conflict analysis: We apply subjective standards, in evaluating others. Our standard of evaluation is influenced, among other things, by how we see the world and the situation in which we currently find ourselves. This filter lies over our observations and often leads to misinterpretation and misunderstanding in our evaluation of others' behavior. In conflict, our lens through which we see the world narrows, making negative interpretations of others' behavior more likely.

This chapter is about different personality types, the influence of the situation on our behavior and how we argue.

3.1 Everyone Is Different: Personalities

Everyone is different. A realization that is not new, but remains amazing and fascinating. Around 7.8 billion different people with different personalities live on this planet.

What it is that we call personality and how personality influences behavior has interested researchers for centuries. Some approaches on the way to the present state of knowledge are described here. It is a short journey through time into the world of attempts to grasp our differences.

Early theories assumed that personality was expressed in people's physical appearance. One approach, developed by the German physician Franz Joseph Gall (1758–1828) and known as phrenology, was based on the idea that we could measure personality by assessing the patterns of bumps on people's skulls. An illustration from an encyclopedia from about 1895 shows a corresponding division of the skull (Fig. 3.1).

Different regions represented different personal expressions. On the basis of the physiological characteristics of the skull, conclusions were drawn about

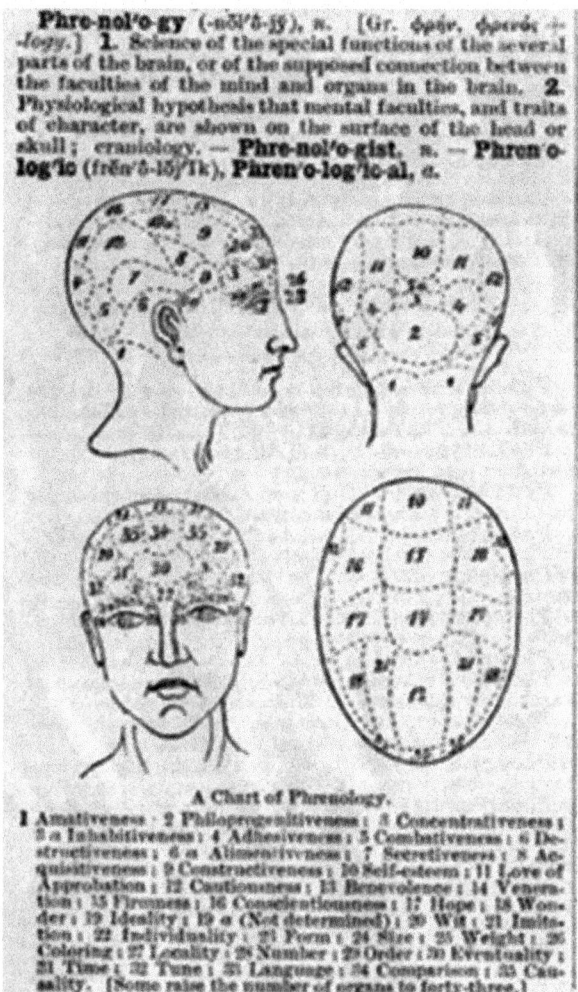

Fig. 3.1 Illustration of the classification of different areas of the skull. Webster's encyclopedia ca. 1895

the personal characteristics. For example, there were areas for self-confidence, courage, cheerfulness, faith, love of children, etc.

In the Victorian era, phrenology was taken very seriously and many people promoted its use as a source of psychological insight and self-knowledge. Machines were even developed to help people with the.

analysis of skulls should help. Later careful scientific research could not confirm this theory of correlations between skull shapes and personality traits. Phrenology no longer plays a role in contemporary psychology (Fig. 3.2).

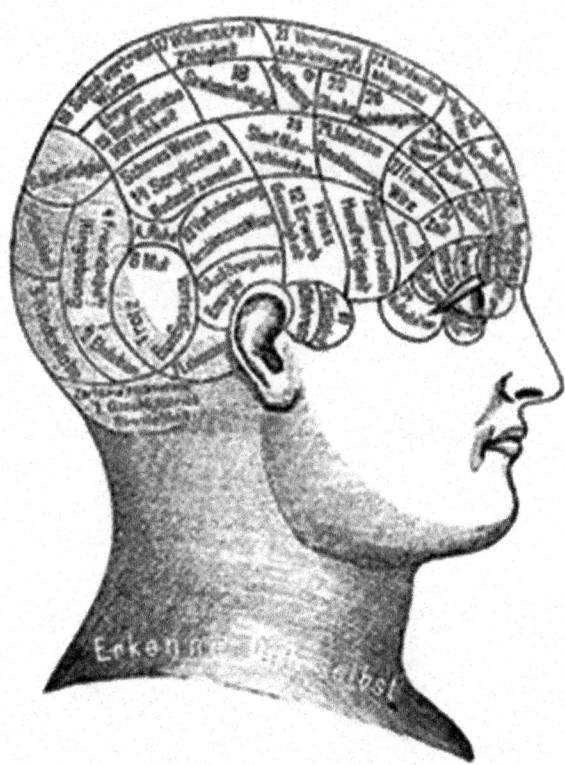

Fig. 3.2 Representation of the human character and faculties. Friedrich Eduard Blitz, neue Naturheilkunde Leipzig, 1902

Another approach is known as somatology. A prominent exponent was the psychologist William Herbert Sheldon (1898–1977). The idea of somatology was based on the idea that we can determine people's personalities based on their physical makeup. Abbreviated, Sheldon argued, among other things, that people with more body fat and a rounder physique (endomorphs) tend to be more assertive and bold, while thinner people (ectomorphs) tend to be more introverted and intellectual. As with phrenology, scientific research has not confirmed the predictive power of this theory. Somatology is not now accepted as valid in contemporary psychology (Fig. 3.3).

Another approach to personality recognition is known as physiognomy, or the idea that it is possible to judge personality by facial features. But even these theories were not empirically actuated and rejected.

Also the humoral theory or pathology, a disease theory of the bodily fluids whose correct mixture or composition is a prerequisite for health, developed in antiquity and valid until the nineteenth century, was linked to the

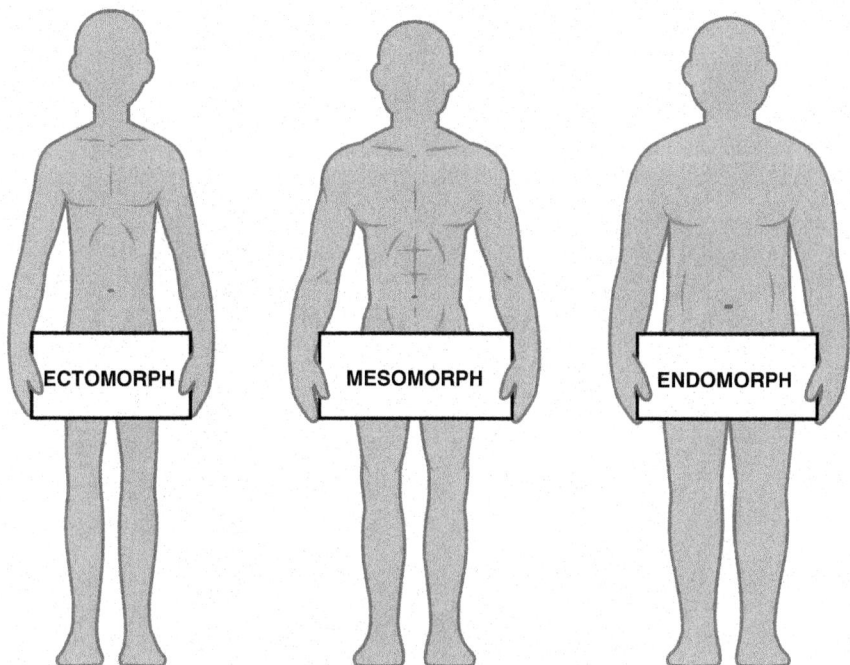

Fig. 3.3 Body types according to William Sheldon

temperaments of people and connected with the four elements doctrine, which goes back to 700 BC.

The fire, was associated with the yellow bile and with a choleric temperament. The earth represented the black bile and melancholy. The air, in this model, is associated with blood and the sanguine temperament, which describes cheerful, lively and frivolous people, and the water is associated with phlegm and a phlegmatic temperament. No evidence could be found for this theory either. Nevertheless, relationships to it can still be found today in esoteric and anthroposophical images of man and teachings, among others (Fig. 3.4).

In current thinking, personalities are characterized by traits that are relatively enduring characteristics that influence our behavior across many situations.

The most popular way to "measure" personality traits is to administer personality tests in which people give self-reports about their own characteristics. Scientists have studied hundreds of traits and have identified some personality traits that have important effects on our behavior. Personality traits such as introversion, friendliness, conscientiousness, honesty, and helpfulness are found to help explain consistency in behavior.

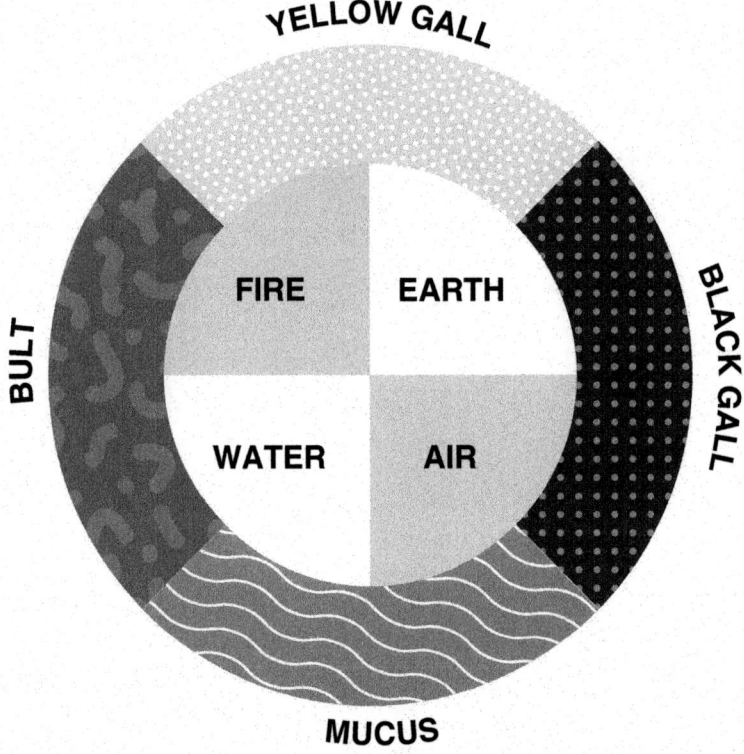

Fig. 3.4 Humour theory linked to four elements

As with intelligence tests, the usefulness of self-assessment measures of personality depends on their predictive reliability: Is the test question likely to elicit reliable responses. The difference between psychologically tested questionnaires and many newspaper self-assessment tests is precisely this. In newspaper tests, the creators usually link an answer to a characteristic. This link is created by an assumption, a hypothesis, which is usually made on the basis of an "everyday psychological" assumption:

For example, you are asked whether you talk to strangers when you are waiting for a train at the station or whether you tend to stay alone and keep your distance. Depending on what you tick, the evaluation could show that you are probably more extroverted or introverted.

This link is based on the assumption of the tester. In this case, for example, he links extroversion with sociability, constructs a corresponding scenario and assumes that people who state that they talk to strangers at the station are more extroverted.

This is a conjecture from everyday psychology but not a reliable test variable, since it has presumably not been adequately tested whether this answer or the behaviour in this described situation actually correlate with extroversion or introversion. In order to make predictions that are as reliable as possible, psychologists conduct many pre-tests when creating scientific tests in order to validate individual questions and the totality of the items. Only when the later test instrument has been tested, i.e. when it has been ensured that a clear majority of extroverted people would actually tick off that they would be more likely to talk to strangers on a railway track waiting for a train, would this question be transferred into an overall catalogue of valid assessment instruments (of in this case extroversion).

Scientifically used personality tests are empirically tested by assessing their effectiveness in terms of the quality of the statement and its stability over time (is the statement valid not only at that moment of the test, but over a longer period of time) and their ability to predict behavior.

The most popular and, according to today's standards, best validated test that uses trait dimensions to describe personalities is the five-factor model (the Big five).

According to this model, there are five fundamental underlying trait dimensions that are stable over time, apply across cultures, and explain a substantial portion of behavior. The five factors in this model are openness to experience, conscientiousness, extraversion, agreeableness and neuroticism (Table 3.1).

The evaluation is carried out in all categories. The result is not an either or result (a person would be either compatible or conscientious), but locates the tested persons on an axis with two poles for each characteristic (e.g. very conscientious – not conscientious at all).

> If you would like to take the test, you can find the questions and a good evaluation free of charge on the Internet on this site The test – Big Five (bigfive-test.com).

Our personality traits influence our actions and thoughts. However, these are also not stable variables.

An Example

When I think about Carla and say, "Clara is a friendly person", I mean Carla is friendly today, she will be friendly tomorrow and most likely next week. I know Carla from our fitness class and this is my experience with her, this is how I experience her: she is accommodating, likes to smile, is open and friendly. If I were to walk home with Carla after yoga

Table 3.1 Summarized and abbreviated presentation of the dimensions of the Big 5 personality test

Dimension.	Description	Examples of behavior predicted by the characteristic
Openness to experience	A general appreciation for art, emotion, adventure, unusual ideas, imagination, curiosity, and a variety of experiences	Individuals who are very open to experiences tend to decorate their homes in an eye-catching and unconventional way. They are also likely to have books on a variety of subjects, a diverse music collection and artwork
Conscientiousness	A tendency to show self-discipline, to act dutifully, and to strive for achievement	People who are conscientious have a preference for planned rather than spontaneous behaviour
Extraversion	The tendency to experience positive emotions and seek stimulation and the company of others	Extraverts like to be around people. In groups they like to talk, assert themselves and draw attention to themselves
Compatibility	A tendency to be compassionate and cooperative toward others rather than distrustful and antagonistic; reflects individual differences in overall concern for social harmony	Agreeable people appreciate getting along with others. They are generally considerate, kind, generous, helpful, and willing to align their interests with those of others
Neuroticism	The tendency to experience negative emotions, such as anger, anxiety, or depression; sometimes called "emotional instability"	Those high in neuroticism are more likely to interpret ordinary situations as threatening and small frustrations as hopelessly difficult. They may have trouble thinking clearly, making decisions, and dealing effectively with stress

class, I would see her arrive home every Tuesday and barely give her dinner-going family a glance. With a petrified expression, she grumbles a "hello" and heads to her room.

What happened, is Carla not a friendly person after all, but even an unfriendly one?

As early as 1968, the psychologist Walter Mischel examined the connection between the situation and the behaviour of people in a study that attracted a great deal of attention .[1]

---

[1] Mischel, Walter: Personality and assessment. 1968.

He concluded that a relatively low correlation exists between the characteristics that a person expresses in one situation or another.

As early as 1928, psychologists Hartshorne, May, Maller, & Shuttleworth[2] studied the correlations between various behavioral indicators of honesty in children. They enticed children to behave either honestly or dishonestly in various situations, for example, by making it easy or difficult for them to steal and cheat. The correlations between children's behaviors were low. It was found that children who behave dishonestly in one situation are not always the same children who behave dishonestly in another situation. Numerous studies have been conducted on moral behavior and character traits based on this.

In summary, the results confirmed that when observing personality traits and behavior based on them, the *situation* has a strong influence.

Another study by Bem and Allen, 1974 actuated the strong situational influence in a study of adults in relation to the traits of dependency, agreeableness, and conscientiousness.[3]

Psychologists have come up with two main assumptions for these low correlations of personality traits in different situations.

One assumption is that our natural tendency to see traits in others leads us to believe that people have stable personalities when in fact they do not. In short, the character traits of others are more prominent in the minds of the people doing the judging than in the behaviors of the people being observed.

This assumption also fits with research showing that people use their own knowledge and conditioning to interpret the world around them. These unconscious schemas color their judgments about the personalities of others.

> **Example**
>
> I was in a serious car accident as a child. This experience has shaped me and to this day I drive very unwillingly and overcautiously. Equipped with this backpack of experience, I often hastily judge others who are driving briskly on the road as reckless or wrongly assume that my passengers also get wet hands from 130 km/h, although in reality they are quite relaxed and enjoying the ride.

To understand the second assumption, I invite you to take a little test.

---

[2] Hartshorne, Hugh, and Mark A. May. "Studies in the nature of character,[part] 1: Studies in deceit: book 1, General methods and results; book 2, Statistical methods and results." (1928).

[3] Bem, Daryl J., and Andrea Allen. "On predicting some of the people some of the time: the search for cross-situational consistencies in behavior." *Psychological review* 81.6 (1974): 506.

> **Important**
>
> First, think of a person you know – your mother, your roommate, a friend, or a classmate. Now choose from answers a/b/c which one describes him or her best.
>
> | 1 | (a) energetic | (b) relaxed | (c) depends on the situation |
> |---|---|---|---|
> | 2 | (a) Sceptical | (b) Confidentially | (c) Depends on the situation |
> | 3 | (a) Calm | (b) Talkative | (c) Depends on the situation |
> | 4 | (a) Intensive | (b) Calm | (c) Depends on the situation |
>
> Now answer the questions again, but this time about yourself.
> What do you notice?

Your answer may be influenced by the fact that you have already read quite a bit about the influence of the situation. This experiment was conducted repeatedly with a large number of subjects. With the following result:

People tend to see more stable and clearly definable character traits in other people than in themselves.

The inventors of this study Richard Nisbett and his colleagues[4] set 840 college students the same task for themselves, for their best friend, for their father, and for the (then famous) news anchor Walter Cronkite.

The vast majority of participants chose response (a) or (b) more often for other people than for themselves, and chose (c) "depends on the situation" more often for themselves than for the other people. These results suggest that people may perceive more consistent traits in others. To exaggerate, we tend to pigeonhole other people more into one personality trait. We observe traits and personality traits in others and interpret them through our lens as we see the world. In doing so, we seem to trust others with less flexibility and variability than we do ourselves. This is the basis for prejudices or false evaluations, among other things.

It happens to us now and then in life that a person "surprises" us.

> **Example**
>
> *Laura was always so shy, I never thought she would give a speech in front of the whole school.*
>
> *I know Mark as a very distant, cool colleague, that he of all people was the only one to visit me in hospital when I broke my leg, I would never have predicted.*
>
> *Ursula was always in such a good mood and cheerful, that she should now have a depression, I can hardly believe.*

---

[4] Nisbett, R. E., Caputo, C., Legant, P., & Marecek, J. (1973). Behavior as seen by the actor and as seen by the observer. *Journal of Personality and Social Psychology, 27*(2), 154–164.

You can probably think of a few examples of this. We see people in a certain situation (in the office, at school, on the tram, in the family) and infer certain personality traits from our observations of the behaviour in this situation. We assume that these are quite stable and underestimate (1) our personal colouring of this assessment and (2) that behaviour changes in different situations.

In conflict, this discrepancy in our assessment comes to a head – we focus on the negative characteristics and behaviors of others in order to create as great a contrast as possible between ourselves and the others. Often we place ourselves on a moral pedestal and evaluate our actions as good, right, morally correct and the behavior of the other as vile, bad or even sick. As the conflict progresses, our perception of the other person's behaviors in this tense situation mixes with our description and perception of their overall personalities.

> **Example**
> *While we see in peacetime that Mrs. Rousé, our usually rather balanced and patient colleague, today exceptionally lost her patience and became louder because she felt attacked by her boss. Does our image of Mrs. Rousé change when we are personally in conflict with her. We see less and less of her even-tempered and patient side, we turn our gaze to her perceived shortcomings, her faults. Mrs. Rousé becomes an unpredictable dragon in our perception. We share this perception with those around us. A downward spiral is set in motion.*

We are dealing with a complex mixed situation: Everyone is different, that is the starting point. Even if we can try to categorize personality types, this cannot make a stable prediction on their behavior. How personality traits show up, e.g. in the form of behavior, is strongly influenced by the situation and by the view from *our* experience-glasses on others.

When we know and recognize our human errors of interpretation, an important step is taken. At best, in a critical situation where we are commenting on or interpreting another person's behavior, we remember to be mindful and careful with judgments about others. Not to be driven or blinded by our spontaneous attributions and thoughts about others, but to reflect on the influence the situation and our own interpretation play. To view others in a nuanced and appreciative way, even in difficult situations, is the fine art of de-escalating and pacifying behaviour.

3.2 What Type of Conflict Am I?

In conflict situations it is easier for us to focus on the others, their shortcomings and mistakes. Yet there is one person in the conflict whom we know best and who may have a part in the tension, the bad mood or the unhealthy communication: Ourselves.

It is worthwhile to look at ourselves and reflect on how we behave in this particular conflict situation and why. Our behaviour and communication are interrelated with the actions and communication of our conflict partners. What we do, say or don't say influences our interaction with others. Like a spiral, the dynamic between us and others spirals upward. Conflict creates a "how-you-make-me-make-you" cycle (Fig. 3.5).

> How direct this correlation is can be tested in a simple self-experiment. Go to the bakery, beam at the staff at the counter and say *"Good morning" in* a very friendly way, possibly with a reference to the good smell in the shop, the nice weather outside. Observe how the short sales contact develops. Repeat the experiment a few days later and keep it short and neutral. What happens now?

Even if you do the experiment not to the baker, but only in your head, two different perhaps even opposite situations arise.

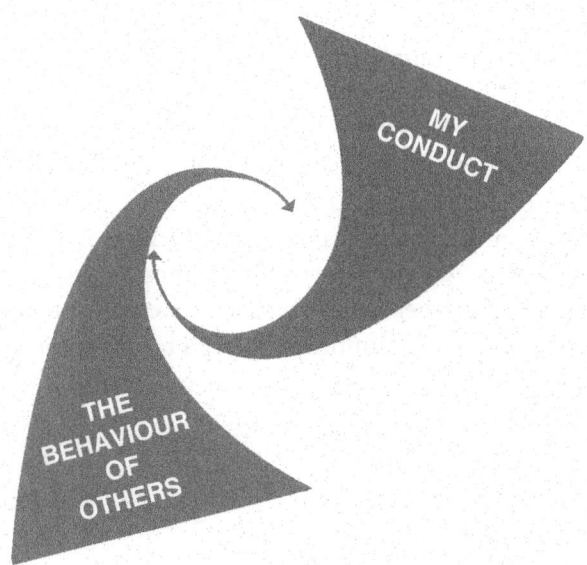

Fig. 3.5 Change reference of our behavior

Another well-known German saying about this interdependence of communication is: **As one calls into the forest, so it calls back.** We all know the principle and yet in the case of conflict we usually do not manage to actively control our calls. We react intuitively to the other person's reaction, adapt to his or her style, and spin ourselves further and further into a bad mood and mutual rejection.

In addition to the spontaneous flight direction of the boomerang of our behavior in a particular tense situation, there are tendencies, preferred trajectories, of how we tend to rule in a conflict situation. Patterns that show up again and again in arguments with others. Those who recognize these patterns, which regularly occur in certain conflict situations (e.g. in conflicts in the family or at work) in themselves or in others, can better adjust to the other person and de-escalate themselves.

Two possible classifications of **conflict types** are described below. The first categorization is derived from personality types and how they argue, the second consideration involves the situation of the conflict and possible resolution options.

Flight, as has already been described, is a common first reaction to an emerging conflict. But what happens after that, when we notice that the conflict giant is getting bigger and bigger. Different types of conflict govern differently in the case of a manifest dispute.

As always in a categorisation, descriptions of different (stereo)types are used, which are described on opposite poles. When trying to situate ourselves, it is not crucial that all the characteristics described apply completely, but that we can identify a tendency within the following different conflict types that applies to us to a greater or lesser extent. First, five conflict types are described: **the extroverted, direct conflict type; the introverted, avoidant conflict type; the detail-oriented, factual conflict type; the intuitive, empathic conflict type; and the analytical, open conflict type.** This is followed by an analysis and reflection of our strengths and weaknesses, for our own further development of our conflict skills. In the third step I give advice on how to deal with the different conflict types in case of conflict.

The Extroverted, Direct Conflict Type

This conflict type usually addresses conflicts openly and directly after a short time and fights for his goals. If this conflict type feels a disagreement, he does not wait long to address it. In his mind, problems can be solved quickly through discussion and argumentation, so he is not afraid to bring up conflicts. Extroverted conflict types are predominantly capable of conflict because they can address conflicts directly and thus prevent them from escalating. Sometimes, however, they lack the sense of the right situation, the right moment to address problems. This type is usually convinced of his own offensive and direct approach, and does not see that this way could intimidate others. For example, when a conflict is brought up in a large group or a topic that is embarrassing or unpleasant for the other person is addressed directly and without much ado. This type of conflict also includes people who tend to want to be right. They tend to insist on their opinion, criticize others and run over the other side with a torrent of words. They also like to blame others for failed conflict solutions.

The Introverted, Avoidant Conflict Type

Conflicts are not addressed openly at first. This conflict type tends to sit out conflicts. In his perception, a conflict discussion often leads to the fact that the dispute only unnecessarily increases or extends and he wants to avoid that at all costs. Clarification of issues is avoided if at all possible. Sometimes this leads to something piling up and then, as in the metaphor of the overflowing barrel, it comes to an overreaction at a trivial occasion. It can also happen that old stories from the past are brought to the table and an atmosphere of "settling accounts" is created. The conflict partners often feel intimidated and surprised by this.

The Detail-Oriented, Factual Conflict Type

Facts count for him. He is firmly convinced that conflicts are best resolved when they are discussed at the factual level. He addresses conflicts at this level directly. He wants all parties to argue factually and objectively. As soon as emotions come into play, the factual level is left and aspects from the relationship level are added, the conversation becomes difficult for him. A frequent response is that arguments on this level are not meaningful and that he will therefore not go into them further. This provides a classification of the importance of the issues from him. His topics on the factual level are relevant, the topics of the others, among others, on the relational level are not. This can be perceived by the conflict partners as a superiority, a communication from above downwards, and consequently often leads to an escalation.

The Intuitive, Empathic Conflict Type

In conflicts, he is concerned with the big picture, with the overall situation. He is on the lookout for the background, interests and motives of the conflict. In the process, the facts play a secondary role. His focus is often more on the others than on himself. His observations and summaries can sound almost psychoanalytical. In conflicts that are mainly on the factual level, this approach can lead to artificially inflating the conflict and complicating matters. Due to his strong focus on the others, his own role, his own part in the conflict often remains in the background.

The Analytical, Open Conflict Type

This type is good at dealing with open criticism. In a conflict situation, he demands openness from others and makes an effort himself to communicate his points of view openly. He is primarily concerned with finding a solution that is *fair to* both sides. A transparent and fair way to achieve this is important to him. He sees the clarification of a conflict like the processing of a project. He proceeds transparently, openly and analytically and expects the same from the conflict partners. He has little use for emotional reactions. Conflict partners who react sensitively to criticism, for example, do not find his understanding. He believes that everything, positive and negative, should be said openly in order to resolve a conflict. This openness can also cause irritation in an intercultural context with people from cultures that perceive criticism as a loss of face and are not familiar with this kind of openness.

> Do you feel reminded of your own behaviour by one or more descriptions? Which aspects of the description are these exactly? Which characteristics of my personal conflict type are positive and how can these be further developed and maintained? Where are the weaknesses in my personal approach to conflict? How can I work on these?

No conflict type is better or worse than the other. As with the personality types, it is not a matter of judging, but of acknowledging the differences, reflecting on one's own weaknesses in conflict behaviour and changing them step by step.

For example, if we find ourselves in the **extroverted, direct** conflict type, then it is important to maintain the open and direct manner with which we address conflicts. In the vast majority of cases, it is good and right to get to the root of conflicts and resolve them before they escalate further or become long-term cold conflicts. However, we can think about how we do that. How we approach others about the conflict. If we have ever observed or received feedback that our counterpart feels blindsided or intimidated by us, then our learning might be in finding the right moment, the right setting, or the right words. It does not help us if we address the conflict directly but catch our conflict partners off guard and go into shock or react by fleeing. Alone we may be able to enforce something or order something to be done, but the interests of the other person are not included in this. In order to resolve a conflict in a sustainable and self-determined way, we need an ally, and that is our conflict partner.

If we identify more with the **introverted, avoidant** type, then we can retain the positive characteristic that in conflicts we probably do not feel the need to escalate the situation and "make a mountain out of a molehill". This is a good thing, we don't argue at all costs, but rather weigh up whether a resolution to the conflict might not be possible by avoiding it, for example, because we know from our experience with this conflict partner that after a few hours the smoke will have cleared. For this type, however, it is important to consider how he can assert his own interests in the long run. The issue of the "overflowing barrel" is also important for this conflict type to reflect on. Do I tend to bottle up issues until I eventually run out of patience? How do I behave then? And what counter-reaction have I already experienced?

For example, you can work on reducing the size of the "inner barrel" or set up an "alarm system" so that there are not so many points piling up, but issues are brought to the table and addressed earlier. If I know that I am an introverted, avoidant type of conflict, I can consciously make sure that I open the floodgates earlier the next time, and that I have strategies in place so that I can do this better.

The **detail-oriented, factual** conflict type can rely on his clarification skills in conflicts over facts. This is a strength. If you have this quality, you can offer it to your team as a moderator, for example, in the workplace. If there is a dispute on the factual level – for example about new developments, project progress or monitoring – this type gladly and efficiently takes over clarification moderation.

The fields of development of this type are on the level of relationships. Hardly any conflict takes place exclusively on the factual level. Acknowledging each other's issues and dealing with issues that lie outside the factual level can help this type to clarify and better deal with other types of conflicts. The first step is knowing that there is a relationship level in addition to the issue level and that the two levels affect each other. This requires a quality of listening in order to understand which interests are expressed by the conflict partners on the relationship level. Chap. 5 deals with techniques to improve listening.

The *intuitive, empathic* type is a good conflict clarifier. His qualities lie in helping others to work out their interests behind the positions and to shed light on the background of the conflict. This conflict type asks a lot of questions, is genuinely interested in people and their stories, and is usually willing to reveal things about himself. If you are such a conflict type, then it probably happens to you frequently that people who are in conflict seek advice from you. They have the feeling that their ears are open to you and they see a deeper interest in the context of the conflict. This quality is also very helpful in clarifying your own conflicts, because the effort to understand others conveys a sense of appreciation to the person you are talking to. Perceived appreciation triggers a positive counter-reaction and has a de-escalating effect.

The challenge for the intuitive types is to sometimes "let the situation be". Not every conflict needs deep clarification and not every dispute has a complex background. Sometimes it helps to fish at the surface of the water and not poke too deep to stir up too much mud. If you identify with the intuitive conflict type, take additional care that you do not look too much at the others in the conflict and interpret their motives and lose sight of yourself in the process.

The **analytical, open** conflict type is robust. He can handle criticism well. This is a very positive quality for self-development and for getting valuable feedback from others about their perception of our actions and behavior. A healthy critical faculties is noticed by others and makes those around us more likely to "dare" to give feedback. We should take feedback as a gift and an opportunity for further development. In conflict discussions, this openness is particularly helpful in finding constructive solutions.

We often infer from ourselves to others. How we react and communicate is familiar, intuitive and close to us. In the stressful situation of a conflict, our thinking and behavior takes a dangerous shortcut – we tend to demand similar qualities and (communication) behavior from others. This type of conflict in particular can overlook the fact that not everyone is so good at dealing with openness and criticism. This is also a sensitive issue in an intercultural context: openness and direct expression of criticism can escalate conflicts and lead to a breakdown in conversation. The interlocutors can get the feeling of being attacked and losing face. This sensitivity, that not all people can understand criticism and directness in the same way and process it culturally or personally, is a learning field of this conflict type.

Self-reflection and self-knowledge are starting points on our path to behavioural change. A conflict (apart from the inner conflict) is not a one-way street, but an interaction with others. The better you can assess the type of conflict management your counterpart tends to, the better you can adapt your conflict resolution strategy to it.

At this point we would like to remind you once again that in your assessment of the conflict personality of others, you unconsciously tend to overestimate your own perceptions and that the situation, in addition to personality traits, has an important influence on our behaviour.

Suppose you have a colleague with whom you have frequent arguments and you see in her characteristics of an extroverted conflict type. Which conflict behaviour would you recommend in this case?

Extroverted conflict types have a direct need to speak. It is easier for them to meet this need and eloquently present their point of view in a very direct manner. It is advisable to be patient and to calmly try to understand the other person's point of view. With people who talk a lot, especially when they are excited, it is advisable to gently force pauses in speech. This can be achieved with the technique of active listening, in which the content heard is summarized in your own words. Through my body language (a slight lean forward, opening of the mouth, raising of a hand, etc.) I give the signal that I would like to hook in. It can feel like a threading on the highway. At the right moment, I take the floor and go with the flow. To do this, I don't switch to counter-talk too soon, but first make an effort to understand what the other person is about. I listen and summarize what I have understood and get feedback on whether what I have echoed is correct. This technique interrupts a torrent of words and structures the conversation.

Due to their outwardly directed character, the **extroverted** conflict type tends to express accusations or complaints about their conflict partners, colleagues, interlocutors or absent third parties very clearly. At this point, consciously try not to react with counter-accusations or justifications, but to lead the conversation back to the factual level. The direct conflict type often acts emotionally himself and is open to arguments on this level. If you feel hurt or annoyed by him in the conversation, then a possible strategy is to reveal yourself and name the feeling.

With an extroverted conflict type a consensus can be found well if the conversation is structured, attacks are not reacted to with counter-attacks and the relationship level is not worked on one-sidedly, but both conflict partners show and name emotions.

If you have an **introverted** conflict type in your close professional or private environment who doesn't say anything for a long time and then has a tendency to explode, it is worth asking regularly whether everything is fine, there are problems somewhere, he or she is feeling well, etc. Consciously show and express openness to argument. *"You can tell me if something bothers you", "it is important to me that we talk regularly about our cooperation", "I am happy about your feedback".* Arrange regular conversations, about your cooperation (if you are a team) or about your relationship, if you are a family or friends. These conversations can take place without any reason, they offer the possibility to release pressure, to better assess the feelings of the other person, to de-escalate if necessary and to avoid a "barrel overflow". With introverted conflict types, pay more attention to body language and learn to hear hints of a brewing storm between the lines.

When it comes to a debate that has been pent up in your counterpart for a long time, it is likely that the introverted conflict type will come up with ready-made solutions that have been worked out "in secret". However, in order to arrive at mutual and tenable solutions, you need to open up the space and include the interests of all parties involved. It can help to make it clear that solutions take time and cannot be unilaterally pre-designed and imposed on others. If you find yourself with preconceived solutions, address that directly and explain what you need to find solutions. It may be that you first want to better understand what the other person's interests are, need space to formulate your own interests or also want to develop options for good solutions together.

If you are arguing with a **detail-oriented** conflict type, it is crucial to make yourself heard on the relationship level as well. Very few conflicts are purely factual. Even in a supposed dispute over facts, there are often deeper issues at stake. One example is conflicts over wage adjustments. On the surface, it's about more or less money at the end of the month-this numerical level is factual. Behind this, however, there may be needs such as appreciation, recognition or security, which are aspects that touch on the relationship level. Other conflicts take place predominantly on the relationship level. The detail-oriented conflict type is hard of hearing on the ear of the relationship level. He sees the facts and keeps coming back to them. All other issues that are not factual in nature, he tries to wipe off the table. In doing so, the detail-oriented conflict type may dismiss the relationship-level aspects and arguments of his counterpart as nonsense. This can be hurtful and frustrating. Deliberately stop your interlocutor at these points and explain to him what you are observing in this conversation and how you feel about it: *"I have revealed something important to you which, from my point of view, is part of this dispute, it hurts me that you do not go into it or that you call this irrelevant. Please also try to hear my issues and not just argue with me on the merits."*

In order to make ourselves heard in the conflict with this type, it can help to overemphasize the relationship level, to address the self-revelation of our own feelings in particular detail and clearly, and to insist as long as we do not feel heard. The point is to strike a balance between our interlocutor's strong focus on the issue level and the relationship level, which plays just as much a role in this conflict. Like a see-saw on the playground, it is not important that our weight, our arguments are whirled into the air at the same time. If we did, we would remain standing, the seesaw at rest and us with our feet in the air. The smooth back and forth, the up and down is important, for a balanced conflict conversation. The factual level takes up space but also the relationship level. The conflict partner has time and space to speak, but so do we.

The **intuitive** conflict type needs a brake in some situations. He likes to look at the big picture and can get lost in side streets. In a conflict resolution the situation then appears more complicated than it actually is. Too many sideshows can interfere with the main event and confuse the parties on their way to clarification. It helps to structure the conflict with the intuitive type. Ask questions about what is at his core, what is most important to discuss, and in what order. Try to leave interpretations out of it and address the obvious problem together first. Concentration should be on each person staying with themselves and not the intuitive conflict type thinking for others, talking along and interpreting statements. If the person you are talking to keeps going down side streets and trying to work out new connections and correlations, express your desire to stay on the core issue. In larger rounds or a more complex topic, an agenda can help. Only when they have a shared understanding of the current topic through this can they look at the bigger picture, if that makes sense for clarification. Structuring and focusing and keeping an eye on your own issues is the challenge of conflict resolution with the intuitive conflict type.

The **analytical** conflict partner is solution-oriented, a constructive, joint clarification can work well.

Your intervention is required when you find that the analyst is getting bogged down in detailed issues. Often the issue is one of procedural justice of the clarification process and the solution. This procedural justice is helpful in facilitating a fair process for all parties and establishing trust in the solution, but it can also become pedantic and distract from the actual conflict. The analyst questions things critically and can handle criticism well himself, but he may lack the empathy to formulate his own criticism in such a way that others do not feel hurt by it. For those who are hurt do not manage to find solutions openly and in mutual trust. Therefore, in tense communication with this type, it is especially important to counteract immediately if you sense that feedback or criticism from your counterpart is hitting an emotional sounding board with you. Try to express how you feel when you are criticized in this way and ask your interlocutor to be appreciative and mindful. Even though the analytical conflict type sometimes overshoots the mark in their directness and need to critically analyze situations, they usually understand objections and requests about the way they communicate and are willing to work on it and respond to others.

This classification of conflict types is based on the characteristics of personalities. There is also another view, which focuses more on the situation and possible solutions of the conflict.

In the following chapter, the ways in which conflicts can be ended and how the different resolution preferences are related to conflict types will be presented schematically.

3.3 What Types of Conflict Resolution Are There?

There are several ways to resolve conflicts.

If one views conflicts in the simplest definition as a clash of different interests, then the way in which the conflict is resolved can be measured by the extent to which one's own interests or the interests of others are taken into account in the process.

Depending on the extent to which the solutions are aligned with one's own interests or **the** interests of others, we distinguish between the conflict resolutions **avoidance, assertion, yielding, compromise and consensus** (Fig. 3.6).

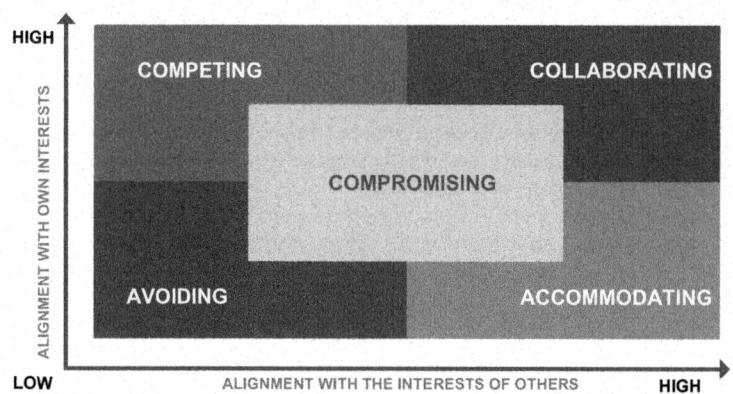

Fig. 3.6 Conflict resolution options. Source: Kilmann, R. H., & Thomas, K. W. (1975). Interpersonal conflict-handling behavior as reflections of Jungian personality dimensions. *Psychological Reports, 37*, 971–980

The Avoidance

It can be useful in some conflicts to avoid the situation. Escape as conflict resolution. A very vivid and simple example of this is our encounter with a shark during our snorkel walk in the sea.

> **Example**
>
> *The shark is hungry. His interest is to eat. We want to enjoy the view of beautiful coral worlds and relax. That is our interest. The shark appears and we decide to escape. We succeed and sit exhausted on the beach. Neither was the shark able to assert its interest and find a tasty meal in us, nor were we able to pursue our interest in continuing to look at the beautiful coral worlds. Nevertheless, escaping was a good conflict resolution for us. Since our original interest was not fulfilled but another interest suddenly took priority, the basic need to stay alive.*

There are other examples where avoiding a conflict can be the right strategy: When we know that we will have nothing more to do with our conflict partners in the future and that asserting our interests at that moment seems less important to us than, for example, having another protracted discussion.

In avoiding a conflict, neither party achieves its real interest, what is actually wanted, intended.

> **Example**
>
> *I remember my own conflict with a real estate agent. I was looking for a suitable apartment and this real estate agent arranged an apartment that I liked. A conflict arose between us in the negotiation about the move-in date and additional costs. Factually, these points would have been settled, we were not far apart. However, the real estate agent had a very insistent manner. For example, he called me several times in a row when I could not answer the phone immediately because I was in a meeting. He would stand outside my office unannounced to discuss details with me and became increasingly uncomfortable with me on a human level. In this case, I preferred avoiding the conflict and my conflict partner. Even though I really liked this apartment and my real interest was to move in there, the relationship level, even if it had been foreseeably short-lived, was so exhausting to me that I decided to give up my dream apartment for it. Even the real estate agent, whose interest was of course to find me this apartment, came up empty in the end.*

Another example of the choice of strategy to avoid conflict can be disputes with people who are mentally confused or in a psychological or physiological exceptional situation. These are morally and humanly difficult situations because, without undermining the self-determination and autonomy of other people, we may be forced to decide whether the interests expressed are feasible, morally defensible, or, for example, do not endanger the person. In turn, our interests may create unnecessary pressure or anxiety in our interlocutors in this exceptional situation of communication, or may simply be misunderstood. If we feel that the preconditions of disputability (e.g. due to a severely limited capacity for self-determination) are not met, then a correct way to proceed may be to avoid conflict.

The Enforcement/Competing

Another conflict resolution is assertion. Another simple example from the animal world, which you have already encountered at the beginning of the book, is the following. They are standing prairie and a tiger appears in front of them. Their interest is to survive. The tiger is hungry. Luckily, they are equipped with stun guns and choose this clarification. Piff puff. The tiger sinks to the ground and they escape with their lives. They have their interests violently served in this case. The tiger sinks into a deep sleep with an empty stomach and wakes up with a still empty stomach from it later.

Another more complex example of enforcement in conflict is hierarchical decision-making.

> ### Example
> *One of my clients is a plant manager and is responsible for an entire production unit with over five hundred employees. She has internalized modern management concepts and tries to work with participation, dialogue and feedback procedures whenever possible. Sometimes, however, it is necessary and important to enforce decisions in the event of conflict. A recent major conflict involved the conversion of a production line. Time was pressing because the parts produced there were needed in a next production step. A production bottleneck has considerable consequences, as subsequent trades cannot continue working, there is a threat of delivery delays and contractual penalties, the warehouses are full and so on. A conflict arose between the new production line and the responsible technician over this changeover. Different interests also played a role here. The technician demanded more conversion time in order to optimise the interfaces between the equipment. The plant manager focused on the overall process and her interest was to start production as quickly as possible. Issues such as appreciation and recognition of the performance and competence of the chief technician also played a role in this conflict. After two meetings, when no resolution was apparent, the plant manager alone decided on the schedule for setting up the production line. She decided in favour of a fast construction and no optimisation of the interfaces. She asserted her interests without further (at least at this point) addressing the interests of the technician. Due to her hierarchical superiority, such a decision was possible.*

Another field of regular decisions by means of enforcement are work areas in which emergency situations are involved. So-called command structures require the possibility to order things and to decide quickly in case of conflict. In doing so, not necessarily own interests are pursued, but acting in the sense of expediency or the assessment of the commander. This is not always in harmony with the troops, but there is an acceptance that this clarification is an efficient one in an emergency, when no time must be lost.

> **Example**
> *I had a mediation with forty firefighters from the volunteer fire department. The conflict was about a tense relationship between the team and their commander. One of the conflict topics was how they treated each other. The conflict ignited because the crew felt unheard and bossed around by their commander even outside of calls for service. In the narrative, they made a clear distinction between the command structures they were familiar with and also accepted during an operation and the club life around it. There they felt that their interests and needs were not heard. Again and again it came to the situation that the commander decided alone after a short time of controversial discussion (for example on which weekend in summer the annual fire brigade festival should take place). Also with questions, who is allowed to the next training or who becomes the new leader of the youth fire-brigade, it was the commander, who asserted its interests and made decisions by order. With the crew this caused a high frustration. The motivation for this voluntary activity decreased. Resignations from the community increased and more and more meetings were held outside the fire station to exclude the commander from discussions among themselves. This steadily deteriorating relationship between the commanders and the troops was eventually reflected in the operations. Even if the troop was trained here to act professionally, it occurred more and more frequently that instructions of the commander for example over the employment order and seat order in the vehicle were not followed any longer. The dispute escalated to such an extent that the dissolution of this voluntary fire brigade was on the cards, which would have had major safety consequences for the community. The issue was resolved after several meetings. Particularly important was the commander's insight that asserting his own interests in the event of conflict causes a lack of motivation and frustration in others in the long run. Those who always put their own interests behind those of others are at some point no longer prepared to give their full commitment to a common cause.*

The Yielding/Accommodating

Another conflict solution is to give in. We stop pursuing our interests and give in to the interests of the other person. As children, we have all heard the saying "the wiser man yields" several times. This saying primarily refers to situations where there is a stalemate due to a back and forth of arguments or bickering. Before, according to the background of this saying, no one has anything, both lose, and the mood is bad, someone gives in so that things can move forward. The reward of giving in, according to the vernacular, is that this act is called being smart. In fact, giving in can be a wise move if, for example, our interests are not that important to us and we do not feel we will be significantly harmed by giving up those interests. We give in and the conflict is thereby ended. The resulting peace may be more important to us than the interest we originally wanted to assert.

> **Example**
>
> *An example here is the argument between Claudia and Franz. The two are a couple and would like to do something together at the weekend. Claudia would like to go cycling because she sits in the office all week and feels like getting some exercise in the fresh air. Franz, on the other hand, would like to spend a weekend together on the couch. He wants to really relax and, if possible, no action. These different interests lead to a small argument over dinner. Both would like to do something together but there is no agreement on the programme. Claudia is impulsive and gets a bit louder during this discussion: "You're turning into a real couch potato, this is not how I imagined our life together" and Franz replies: "Your fitness mania is becoming a burden. Is it really no longer possible to relax with you?" Slowly the argument builds up. Both go to bed in a bad mood and at a loss for words. The next morning, it is Saturday, there is still no clarification in sight and the mood is in the cellar. The weekend threatens to be unpleasant and full of conflict. Then Claudia suddenly gives in. She agrees to spend Saturday on the sofa. Even though this doesn't satisfy her original interest, she'd rather give in and spend some quality time with Franz than get bogged down and end the weekend in a fight.*

In this example, there is a trade-off between what I give up when I give in and the situation that arises when I don't give in.

For one situation or another, this may be the wiser course. If this situation occurs more often or if it develops into a pattern of a relationship, then there is a danger for the giver to get into a role in which he or she constantly renounces own interests. Since our interests are connected to our needs, to renounce them is also to act against our needs.

> **Example**
>
> *If we go back to the example of Claudia and Franz, it is quite understandable and sympathetic that Claudia gave in in this case in order not to poison their weekend together with an argument. But if this were to become a pattern, it would mean that if Claudia wanted to spend time together with Franz, she would probably ride her bike less than she would like. Her need for exercise, for physical activity after an office week, would thus not be met. In the long run, this could make Claudia feel unbalanced and unwell.*

Of course, you as a reader can now think of many options how this problem could be solved. Claudia could go cycling alone or do this on another day. But that is not the point here. The point is to make clear that giving in, which becomes a regularity, in a relationship in private or at work can lead to us not being able to fulfil our needs and thus experience a restriction.

The Compromise

This conflict resolution is one of the most common: the compromise. An example from our childhood is the dispute about "sleeping upstairs".

> **Example**
> At the sleepover party with the girlfriend, the center of attention is a bunk bed with two tiers: downstairs and upstairs. The conflict is easily explained: both kids want to sleep on top. It's more exciting, there's an overview of the room, it feels like an adventure. But upstairs is only one place and the parents don't allow both children to sleep upstairs because they fear one might fall off. Both kids have one interest: sleeping upstairs. Before the mood tips over, the mother intervenes and asks the children if they might find their own solution. The solution is quickly found: today the guest sleeps upstairs and next time it's the other way round. So that the order is not forgotten, the children write a small note which they hang on the wall.

In this solution, the interests of both children are not fully met. If they could wish for something, both would always sleep upstairs. But they are partially fulfilled, namely 50/50. Examples of such compromises are numerous in our lives. We are trained to act reciprocally: *I give you something, then you give me something.* We learned in our childhood that this negotiating and meeting in the middle is frequently and easily applied in everyday life. Also the so-called bazaar- negotiation plays itself out after this pattern. Everybody moves away from his position a little bit, the seller decreases his price and the buyer comes towards him from his minimum offer. This "meeting in the middle" are classic compromises.

The Consensus/Collaboration

There is still one type of conflict resolution in which both parties fulfill their interests as fully as possible. This is consensus. The idea here is not to negotiate against each other or to meet in the middle, not to give in or to impose something unilaterally, but to find a common solution that is ideal for all parties. Admittedly, this sounds like something out of a fairy tale with a happy ending. Two parties argue and in the end they both win? This kind of solution is described in one of the most famous negotiation concepts (the Harvard concept[5]). The following example from my practice comes to mind:

> **Example**
>
> *It was a dispute between two companies. A supplier and a final producer. The conflict arose because the supplier could not deliver a component in the planned quantity on a certain date. Contractual penalties were involved and even the cancellation of the entire order. This dispute was critical for both companies and, as a consequence, even threatened their existence. In order to understand what was at stake for both companies, the interests behind the contractual formulations were first worked out. It quickly became clear that the manufacturing company had made further delivery commitments to end customers and resellers that were in danger of not being met if the supplier's components did not arrive on time. The supplier was having problems procuring raw materials and hence the delay in delivery. The management tried everything to procure the required raw material by other means in order to deliver on time after all. Unfortunately, these efforts were not successful. In the course of the discussion it became clear that it is not at all crucial for the producing company that the entire quantity is delivered on a certain date. On the contrary, it came out that there was another problem of storage capacity at the producing company that was independent of this. The subcontractor was able to meet the delivery date for a smaller quantity without any problems and, knowing of the storage capacity problems of its customer, it was offered to arrange the supply chain differently in the future so that the parts would be delivered to the manufacturing company in smaller quantities and with a time delay. The management of the manufacturing company, it emerged in further discussion, has a contact with a supplier of the required raw material and offered to establish this contact so that the raw material-dependent supply risk was minimised. Since the manufacturer itself purchases a large quantity of the raw material and was therefore able to negotiate a better price, the two managing directors wanted to try to bring this price advantage into the joint negotiation. In the end, a consensual solution was found:*
>
> - *Part of the component was delivered on time, which was sufficient to meet the customer's other delivery obligations.*
> - *The supply chain was changed so that the producing company could optimise its storage capacity.*
> - *In the future, the procurement of raw materials will go hand in hand, which will have a favorable impact on the price.*
> - *The business relationship is on a firm footing, the management has seen that cooperative solutions are possible among themselves, which strengthens the long-term cooperation.*

---

[5] The original title is "Getting to yes" and was written in the 1981. Fisher, Roger; Ury, William; Patton, Bruce The Harvard Concept. 2018.

This is an example of a typical win-win solution. Another very well known example is the two sisters and the oranges.

> **Example**
>
> *Two sisters are fighting over an orange. Both claim to need the whole orange. After some back and forth, they can't agree. They compromise and each of the sisters gets one half of the orange. In the evening, the two sisters discover something amazing. There is half an orange peel and half a pulp in the trash can. What had happened? One of the sisters wanted to bake a cake and only needed the grated peel. The other sister wanted to squeeze a juice and needed only the pulp. If the two sisters had discussed their interests, a consensus would have been possible: One could have used the peel of a whole orange and the other had a whole orange to squeeze a juice.*

The examples show that consensual solutions are not necessarily obvious. It takes work for the conflicting parties to get there. And it takes creative solutions in some cases to meet all the interests of all parties. We also call these creative solutions a "pie enlargement." Not only is the pie that is already on the table divided up, but it is enlarged. Additional fruit or cream is added. This enlargement of the mass to be distributed leads to the possibility of both parties achieving their interests and thus emerging as joint winners. In pure distributional conflicts, such as the division of a certain amount of money between two parties, this is not readily possible. What one gives away, the other gets in addition. Only if the mass to be negotiated is increased and new solution options are worked out together can a consensus be reached in the end.

From these five possible solutions and all the nuances that lie in between, corresponding conflict types can be derived. As already mentioned, this is not about static personality assignments, but about tendencies and preferences of the individual in dealing with conflicts. There are people who tend to avoid the conflict and the conflict partner in conflict situations – the avoiders. Others tend to assert themselves. Still others are more likely to compromise, tend to give in or think in a consensus-oriented way. The situation plays a role and the context of the conflict, but there are personal patterns and recurring behavior in conflict situations.

The conflict types have different strengths and weaknesses:

A strength in dealing with conflicts of an **avoider** is that the danger of a spontaneous escalation of the conflict is low. Short-circuit reactions are rare and as a rule he or she does not offend anyone. The weakness of personalities who avoid conflict is that it takes a great deal of effort to avoid the conflict. Excuses often have to be found, even to the point of denial. In addition, the conflict usually does not resolve itself and remains and persists. Like a boomerang, it keeps coming back and there is a danger that the conflict will continue to escalate in the long term and be perceived by the avoider as increasingly unpleasant. One's own interests fall by the wayside, which in the long run can mean a restriction of one's needs, the quality of one's relationship with others, or one's own possibilities and desires.

The **assertive** conflict type likes to take the initiative and is interested in making decisions. His interaction in conflicts provides clarity and resolves the conflict in a direct way. These are important strengths and qualities that this type brings. The weaknesses are that assertion and control cost a lot of strength and energy. Because he allows few other opinions to stand, he risks a reciprocal, constructive relationship with others. On those around him, this assertiveness can have a dominant effect and cause feelings of inferiority and withdrawal, among other things.

He or she who gives **in** leaves room for the other person, which can be a strength. He or she usually reacts flexibly, does not overdrive or overburden the other person and does not stir up renewed conflicts with his or her peaceful manner. On the other hand, the conflict resolution of giving in is often to one's own detriment. This abandonment of one's own interests can even lead to self-denial. The conflict remains longer and can grow to internal conflicts, because the own interest was not consistently represented.

The **compromiser** is interested in solutions. He has inner room for negotiation and can therefore react flexibly. At the end of a dispute with a type who can compromise well, there is often a constructive solution. Nevertheless, there are also weaknesses of this conflict type. He may be too quick to settle. According to the motto rather something than nothing at all, he renounces a part of his interests, which could possibly have been achieved with a closer look and more intensive discussion.

The **cooperative** conflict type is interested in solutions. It is important to him that all interests are taken into account. This strong orientation towards the interests of the other person and equally towards one's own interests, lays a good foundation of the relationship with the partner. A disadvantage of consensus can be that no clear decisions are reached. Decision-making can take a long time because options and possible solutions are weighed up and evaluated and decided upon in sometimes lengthy processes. Sometimes the

Conflict type	Strengths	Weaknesses
Enforcer	• takes the initiative • is interested in a decision • provides clarity • resolves the conflict	• Control costs strength and energy • Dislikes other opinions • risks the relationship with the other • can cause feelings of inferiority and withdrawal in the other person
Avoider	• there is no escalation • there are no "knee-jerk reactions • don't bump into anyone	• high effort to avoid the conflict (excuses, denial) • Conflict remains • Own interest falls by the wayside
Yielder	• leaves room for the other • can react flexibly • does not overstrain the other person • does not stir up renewed conflict	• Solution is often at own expense • Self-denial • Conflict remains longer because the own interest was not consistently represented
Compromiser	• is interested in a solution • has room for negotiation • can react flexibly • resolves the conflict	• may be "satisfied" too quickly • Abandons part of one's interests
Cooperative	• is interested in a solution • respects all interests • is interested in the relationship with the other Person	• Danger no r clear decisions • Decision making may take too long

Fig. 3.7 Model according to Kenneth Wayne, Thomas. Thomas-Kilmann Confict Mode Instrument. 2002. Schwarz, Gerhard: Konfliktmanagement/Konflikte erkennen, analysieren, lösen. 2014

processes take so long that external conditions have changed and need to be renegotiated again (Fig. 3.7).

Our preference for action in conflict is related in part to personality types (big 5). For example, there is research showing that high **extraversion** personalities tend to be more self-interested **and** therefore more **assertive** and **cooperative**, whereas, for example, high **agreeableness personality** types tend to be more *compromising*.

And people with high values of **openness,** seem to prefer **compromise** and **consensus.**[6]

We evolve in life, learn, and are confronted with experiences that change the way we see the world, our relationships, and our conflicts.

I have encountered many people in my practice who have consciously changed the way they deal with conflict (Fig. 3.8).

---

[6] Study by Ma Zhenzhong: Exploring the Relationships between the big five, personality factors, conflict styles and bargaining behaviour, IACM 18th annual conference 2005.

Example

I remember a man who fled conflict all his life. He grew up in a family where there were many conflicts. The father was an alcoholic and the mother led a double life. None of this was addressed. The well-off bourgeois family had to mime sunshine to the outside world, even when thick storm clouds were gathering inside. Later he broke off contact with his best and only childhood friend. A small story piled up into an argument, he didn't want to confront it and fled the conflict and henceforth the friend. He later changes jobs twice due to conflicts he felt unwilling to actively resolve. He married and had a child. When conflicts arose in the marriage about raising children and taking responsibility, he was on the verge of running away from this as well. He found it difficult to go to mediation. His first words were that he was here for the sake of his son. In the clarification process, this very analytical and sensitive man consciously recognized for the first time his pattern of avoiding conflict. He took the time to retrace the major conflicts of his life and in almost all of them he behaved similarly: escape. He described himself like the three familiar monkeys- ears closed, mouth shut, and eyes closed. As he reflected on this pattern, the desire grew within him to work on it. He learned through conflict coaching how to confront conflict, how to walk on thin ice verbally in a way that he still felt comfortable with, and developed techniques for himself to face conflict. He made a start with his old school friend. After many years of silence, he sought out contact. Strengthened by this very positive experience of regained friendship, he now actively approaches conflicts and has developed from a conflict avoider to a person who, depending on the situation, also seeks compromise or consensus.

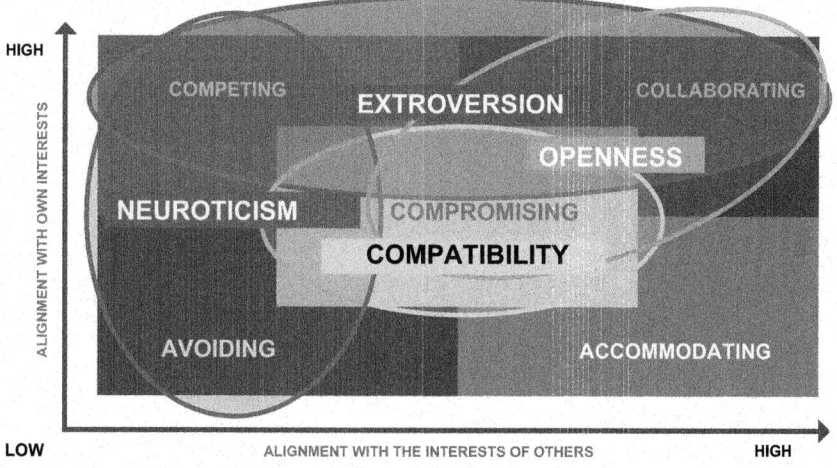

Fig. 3.8 Relationship between personality type and conflict type

This chapter was about the individual level, how we as unique people with our special way deal with conflicts in different situations. However, there is a higher level. A social psychological view: What happens to people when they are in a conflict? There are patterns that play out that can be generalized and have nothing to do with our individual imprint.

I call this, the spiral of conflict.

4

The Spiral of Conflict

When you stand inside a spiral and start running, you first spin yourself. Slowly you move further and further away in endless loops and run laps that get bigger and bigger. You have already learned about the conflict stages, there too the conflict increases stage by stage, the path is exhausting and becomes more arduous. These conflict stages and also the aura of the conflicts play a role in the inner conflict spiral that opens up as soon as we are in conflict.

This chapter is about: what happens to us when we enter into conflict?

As soon as we notice that a difference of opinion, a difference of interest, a small dispute cannot be settled, that we cannot simply tick it off and put it aside, we are at the starting point of the conflict spiral. Reliable signs of an incipient conflict show up in psychological, mental changes and later in physical symptoms. We think about this conflict more and more often, thought gyroscopes develop, which we can stop only with difficulty. These thoughts are not positive. They weigh us down. When they come, our moods worsen. When they come, the corners of our mouth go down and we feel depressed. When they come, we feel like we are being controlled by them. The person we are in conflict with, we try to avoid as much as possible.

> **Example**
>
> *We also avoid the neighbour, with whom we have had a dispute for two years over the pruning of trees on the boundary of the property, in the stairwell. When we hear the door of his apartment open, we prefer to wait five minutes longer behind our closed door before we also leave the house.*

If we cannot avoid our conflict partner, then every encounter with him or her makes us feel uncomfortable. We are tense, excited, perhaps nervous or uncertain, and often feel afterwards that we have behaved unnaturally. We then consider whether we may have been too friendly or said something we didn't mean to say. Our introspection is heightened and encounters are analyzed more critically and closely than in peaceful times.

Often those affected also feel conflicts physically: they cannot sleep well, depending on the type we eat particularly much or particularly little, stomach ache, rising blood pressure, migraine and heart palpitations. When we are at the starting point of the conflict spiral – inside the vortex, we feel that we have a conflict. At this point there are two possibilities: Either we make a big jump out or we start running down the spiral.

The big leap takes place through the clarification of the conflict. As already described with the conflict levels, at the beginning of a conflict we are often still able to leave the (devil's) circle on our own. To do this, the argument, anger, or whatever we call it that catapulted us to this place must be clarified. Clarification is successful when the distressing symptoms or negative feelings have largely disappeared. When we can meet our neighbor in the stairwell again and our mental merry-go-round has come to a halt.

If there is no clarification in the form of reconciliation, debate or joint solution at this starting point, then we start running. We go round in circles in the spiral of conflict and our perception changes. Three qualities of perception are affected: feeling, thinking, wanting.

4.1 Change in Thinking

First of all, the perception towards the situation we are in and our conflict partner changes. The deeper people are in conflict, the more they see their environment in black and white contrast. Outside of a conflict situation, we make nuanced judgments about our interlocutors and our surroundings. We are observers in our lives. When all is well, we see events in many shades. In a conversation, we perceive things on different levels that influence our thinking. We hear what the other person is saying. We see how he behaves and automatically compare what he says with the facial expressions of the other person. If we know our conversation partner better, then we also perceive more intimate things, such as their mood, a change in the way they talk or whether they have been to the hairdresser. All this information flows together unconsciously and influences our thinking about the situation and about the person we are talking to. When we are not in a conflict situation, we perceive things without actively evaluating them. For example, we hear that our conversation partner is speaking softly, we see that he looks happy or has a nice hairstyle. Even if this information is not relevant in the context of the conversation. If, at the end of the conversation, someone were to ask us what the person we were talking to looked like, we might remember that they had a nice hairstyle without actively thinking about it. In conversations outside of conflicts, there are also irritations: for example, our interlocutor says she is fine, but looks very sad. This discrepancy between what is said and the body expression causes an irritation, a doubt. Perhaps this observation continues to preoccupy us after the conversation. We think about why she looked sad. The perception we had in this conversation influences our thinking. Normally, thinking about people is shaped by different aspects, depending on how close or distant the people involved are to each other, how close their relationship is, and how sympathetic you are to the person. Thinking in peacetime is differentiated. We perceive some things and forget them immediately, we perceive others and do not evaluate them, and we think about some things.

When irritation is experienced in a communication, an inner process of evaluation and consideration starts. This is what we have learned to do – to assess situations, to consider decisions, to work out the advantages and disadvantages of an undertaking. In times of peace, these two voices have a balancing effect: they are often described as the voices of heart and reason or associated with little angels and little devils sitting on the shoulder. Let's go back to the situation in which the person we were talking to said she was fine, but looked sad to us. Then it could sound something like this in us. Voice 1: "This woman is not honest with you, she said something and doesn't mean it". Voice 2: "Now don't be so skeptical. She'll already have her reasons for not wanting to say here and now why she feels bad."

Through this interplay, differentiation in thinking arises. However, the inner dialogue has its limits in "healthy" people. Our brain reacts strictly when the voices become too loud or when too many inner voices speak in confusion. For if we had a chorus of inner voices weighing pros and cons, pros and cons, in every conversation we have and in every situation we find ourselves in, we would be incapable of action and completely overloaded. In peacetime, our inner voices are adjusted. They speak when there is room for them and remain silent when there is no need.

Very different in conflict:

We feel irritation and uncertainty and the greater these become, the louder the voices in our head. What is said is no longer simply perceived, but interpreted, twisted and turned. In addition, there are emotions that influence our thinking. We feel hurt, angry, sad, or gloating. These feelings override our view of what is happening. A storm breaks out in our head. The situation is aggravated by the fact that perceptions, thoughts, opinions, attitudes, wishes and intentions are often in conflict with each other. For example, we perceive that our conflict partner has perfectly good arguments for his position, but we do not want to allow this because we have formed the opinion. In psychology, this is called cognitive dissonance:

When two cognitive elements contradict each other and one expresses the opposite of the other in some respect, dissonance occurs. These states of inner discord are perceived as unpleasant and create inner tensions that urge to be overcome. One way to relieve these tensions would be to get along. But this is easier said than done. We are no longer at the starting point of the conflict spiral and our perception has already changed. And not only ours, but also the other's.

Another way to reduce the tension is to keep the dissonances in our brain as small as possible. To do this, we have built up behavioral mechanisms over the course of our lives. Repression and running away, for example, are among the mechanisms to reduce inner tension, at least in the short term. In conflict something else happens, we change our thinking and no longer allow actions, behaviours or statements of the other person to be interpreted positively. Instead we form a contrast thinking: "You bad, I good". Our thinking changes according to the principle: Everything the other person does or doesn't do, we put into the category: "Typical, again he acts this way or that way, I didn't expect it any other way, that's exactly where the problem lies, etc."

We protect ourselves from too much cognitive clutter, which would paralyze us from making other decisions unrelated to the conflict. Liber keeps us consistent in our view of the other. The perfidious thing about this protection is that it blinds us to things that don't fit into our (conflict -) picture. This means that even if our conflict partner intentionally takes a step towards us because he would like to end the conflict and do something good, we no longer see this effort or even interpret it as hidden manipulation.

In a conflict between two colleagues I could observe this dynamic.

> **Example**
>
> *Two department heads Mr. Henkel and Mr. Bach have not seen eye to eye for some time. One issue that has been bothering Mr. Henkel and that he has never expressed to other colleagues or his supervisor is a perceived injustice. Mr. Bach has a company car – as does Mr. Henkel – but Mr. Bach's company car is one category better than Mr. Henkel's. And this despite the fact that Mr Bach joined the company two years after Mr Henkel. Mr. Henkel never asked or discussed why his colleague was given the better car by the company; after all, he didn't want to be seen as the envious one, but he had been feeling it for months. In addition, Mr. Henkel is an outspoken car lover and Mr. Bach's car has been a secret dream of his for years. But this is by no means the only issue between the two and the mood has been in the cellar for some time. Mr. Bach, who has actually always found Mr. Keller congenial and, when he was still new to the company, had a good, long talk with Mr. Keller about cars over lunch, a passion he found bonding, didn't quite understand how the conflict actually came about. His wife advised him to simply approach Mr. Henkel and be friendly, perhaps the conflict would resolve itself. Mr. Bach thought for a while about how he could do that. Mr. Henkel reacted coldly to a friendly "Good morning", and he turned down an invitation to lunch with the excuse of an important appointment. Mr. Bach had a couple of car collector magazines that he knew would interest Mr. Henkel. He wrestled his way, after much inner tossing and turning, to put these car magazines in Mr. Henkel's pigeonhole with a little note on them that they came from him. Mr. Henkel found the newspapers and boiled over with rage: "That's typical, he picks at my wounds. Now he's also putting car newspapers in my locker to rub my nose in it one more time about how great his car is." Malice, spitefulness and gloating: that was how Mr Henkel interpreted the gesture. Mr. Henkel's wife asked him at home whether this gift might not be meant in a nice way. Mr. Henkel became even angrier and the dinner ended in a quarrel.*

In this situation, Mr. Henkel was already so deep in the conflict spiral that it was not possible for him to recognize this well-intentioned gesture by Mr. Bach. Not even the variant "maybe he could have meant it well" was allowed by Mr. Henkel in his thinking. By his interpretation that Mr. Bach's gesture was malicious and spiteful, he reduced the dissonance in his mind. For this supposedly malicious action, fits consistently into the image that Mr. Henkel has of Mr. Bach.

Consistency is another psychological factor that influences our perception in the event of conflict. Consistency here means a firmness in one's own opinion. We strive not to behave like "flags in the wind", but to stick to what we have said and established. Even as a child, we are praised for finishing things, following through on plans and pursuing plans. In conflict, this consistency is just as pronounced. Through consistency, we also achieve relief from cognitive dissonance. Mr. Henkel has been thinking negatively about Mr. Bach for several months, this consistency in thinking, he maintains. This is not a conscious process, but a psychological "program" that runs automatically. Every disturbance of this consistency is first tried to ignore or to integrate into the own thinking pattern. As in the example of the two department heads. An observer from the outside would at least have considered the possibility that the magazines they brought with them could be a message of peace. Mr. Henkel, who is conflicted, does not have that option. This gesture has the potential to destroy his inner image and automatically it is reinterpreted into an action that fits the overall weather situation. Mr. Henkel has moved on in the spiral of conflict, his thinking has changed.

4.2 Change in Feeling

The next perceptual quality that changes is feeling. Normally, in the course of our maturation process of growing up and later in adult life, we have developed the capacity for empathy. Empathy is the capacity for compassion and empathizing with the feelings and experiences of others: feeling as if they were our feelings without leaving the "as if" quality. Empathy is a fundamental human quality that enables us to build and sustain human relationships.

Scientists believe that empathy is neurobiological: observing and imitating the emotions of others evokes almost the same patterns of arousal in us as if we were feeling the emotions ourselves. These resonant systems in the brain, are called mirror neurons. Those neurons are already sending out signals when we observe an action. The resonance that is generated in us is similar to the situation in which we ourselves feel these emotions. As we age, our ability to empathize with others changes. Researchers have found that as people age, they become somewhat worse at recognizing others' emotions by facial expressions, for example. At the same time, people who are more experienced in life are better able to develop empathy when they hear about bad experiences or receive verbal information about the other person's feelings. Is it important to distinguish between empathy and compassion versus pity. Whereas empathy is usually based on our own experiences and triggers a mirrored reaction in us, pity is developed because we see someone in distress, for example, without really being able to empathise with how they feel. e.g. starving people or those injured in war. Putting ourselves in the other person's shoes, interests and needs enables us to better understand our counterpart. This ability plays an important role in communication with each other. We normally react to the feelings of our interlocutors with the desire to understand them. In addition to intuitive empathy, which can be seen, for example, between parents with babies, or when comforting someone when they are crying, or when we calm someone down because we sense that they are upset, there is also a conscious search for the other person's emotional state. By asking questions, for example, in order to better understand what is going on inside him. We don't always succeed in intuitively and spontaneously sensing how our fellow human beings are feeling right away. Sometimes it takes more information about the feelings of the other person to build empathy for them.

Empathy is considered in psychology as a prerequisite for moral action.

In conflict, the performance of the nerve cells (mirror neurons) that trigger our empathy suffers. Also in stressful situations or in situations in which we ourselves are in pain or on the run, for example, the function of the mirror neurons is shut down.

In the case of conflict, this happens piecemeal and analogously to the degree of escalation and our involvement in the conflict. The more we get into the conflict spiral, the less empathy we feel. This loss of empathy, acts like a fire accelerant. For example, we see that our counterpart is stressed or sad, but it doesn't trigger a response in us. If we revisit the link between empathy and moral action, we better understand why people are capable of violence or killing in highly escalated conflicts, such as war. Among other situational and psychological effects, the mirror neurons are "turned off." The suffering of others no longer reaches us and reaches us.

The lack of empathy in conflicts leads to the fact that we understand the other less and less and the perception of our counterpart changes drastically. In this situation, we can no longer reliably call up empathy, which psychologists also call a primary phenomenon (inherent in us). Something in us resists feeling the feelings of the other person. As with the change in thinking, we also strive for consistency in our feelings. It doesn't fit when we suddenly soften at the tears of our rivals. People in conflict can regularly be seen to turn away from each other when one of them displays feelings that would trigger empathy in times of peace. For example, sadness. In doing so, they want to prevent a resonance from arising within them at the sight of tears. This resonance to also become sad and the spontaneous reaction to even want to comfort the other does not fit the conflict program.

> **Example**
>
> *A drastic case of lack of empathy, I could observe in a conflict between brother and sister, who ran a family business together, until it came to worse and worse quarrels among themselves. The two accused each other of setting wrong priorities and of betraying each other. Their perception of each other changed step by step. Formerly siblings with a good connection who ran a business became disputants who, they both said, no longer recognized each other. Their emotions were different. While the brother was more likely to feel anger, frustration and a lack of understanding, the sister was more likely to react with offense, coldness and hurt. The argument reached a point where the two could not communicate, much less keep company with each other. And then something fateful happened. The sister developed cancer, a brain tumor with a very poor prognosis. This seriously changed their professional situation. The two had to sit down together to talk about a solution for the future. The sister, who had teenage children, felt thrown off the track of life. She no longer felt like arguing, she was in a hurry to find solutions, for the company and her family. Even in this drastic situation, the brother was unable to build up compassion for his seriously ill sister. He got involved in mediation, but initially behaved coldly and intransigently. He did not want to hear about the diagnosis and always pointed out that the problems did not start with it, but that there was a reason why he was so angry and that a diagnosis like this did not change anything.*

For the reader this may sound very harsh, we tend to condemn this man for his behavior, because even the narration of the fate of the sister, triggers something in us. For some it is pity, we understand cognitively how bad such a diagnosis must feel, but feel nothing ourselves because this woman is fictional to us and/or we don't know the situation. Others already feel empathy even with this narrative. Something in you resonates with this story. Perhaps it is your own fear of experiencing something similar. Perhaps you have experienced something like this and it reflects familiar feelings in you.

> **Example**
>
> *In the case of the brother or sister, it took a longer period of conflict resolution for empathy to return in the brother. This return of empathy also marked the turning point in this conflict.*

4.3 Change in the Will

The next change in perception is in wanting. In peacetime, what we want is negotiable and flexible. We have more or less concrete ideas about what we would like to have, for example where we would like to spend the next holiday, how much money we would like to earn, which city we could move to and in which family form we would like to live. Wanting is shaped by needs and interests. It is therefore negotiable and flexible, because needs and interests change and what was originally wanted is not (any longer) the first preferred option in view of changed circumstances.

> **Example**
>
> *For example, the original plan to live in a city apartment in a big city could be pushed into the background because we have found the great love who lives on the farm in the country. The need that originally manifested our desire to live in the city could have been not to feel lonely, to have many people around us, to be in the middle of life. With great love, however, comes another hitherto unknown need: To enjoy togetherness and tranquility, and perhaps to build a nest for a family.*

This shift in needs does not usually happen overnight, but it does permanently change what we want.

> **Example**
>
> *In this case of great love, it may be a process of negotiation to give up our once chosen lifestyles, allow the change in need, and move in new directions. Perhaps friends and family have wondered about this change in what we want. However, if we explain to them what new needs and interests are behind it, they will certainly understand this step (better).*

Behind our wants are needs. The American social psychologist Abraham Maslow[1] illustrated these in a pyramid. In his model, needs are categorized into levels. At the bottom of the human needs pyramid are the basic physiological needs: Eating, Drinking, Sleeping, Breathing, Procreation, and Excretion. Only when these are satisfied, Maslow says, do new needs arise. The next level satisfies our quest for security: physical security, the security of our family, our health, the security of our property, work, and the security of our resources (house and yard).

Once we have also achieved these needs, then we take care of love and belonging. This includes categories such as friendship, family, and physical intimacy.

---

[1] Maslow, Abraham (1954): *Motivation and Personality.* Harper, New York.

Once we have climbed these three levels of need, we belong to the privileged people on our planet. But the wanting does not stop at this point. Now needs for appreciation and recognition arise. In this category fall respect for others and respect from others, self-confidence, self-esteem, and success. Finally, at the top of the pyramid of needs, we desire self-actualization: creativity, education, spirituality and philosophy-in short, the pursuit of a "better" me.

The attainment of needs always takes the path from the bottom to the top in the pyramid model. A person who is hungry and has no roof over his head will probably not feel the need for further education, but will concentrate on ensuring that his basic needs are met. Only when the basic physiological needs and security have been achieved is there a certain permeability of the upper layers of needs (Fig. 4.1).

There are also criticisms of this model, which I would like to mention briefly here. Contrary to Maslow's analysis that the needs would only be fulfilled in the order (from bottom to top), other authors also see other directions of movement. In their view, stages can be skipped and a way back is also possible. If, for example, we fall seriously ill or a pandemic breaks out, basic needs come to the fore again. Moreover, this model is very Western. In other cultures, needs can be experienced with a different level of importance.

Important to understand the dynamics of conflict is that our wants, our interests are linked to underlying needs.

In the spiral of conflict, wanting changes. We lose flexibility in our wanting and our expressed wanting moves away from the underlying needs. In conflicts the focus is on positions and not on the underlying interests. To illustrate this, I describe the example of a conflict at work, between a successful, well-paid manager and the management.

Example

One day, unexpectedly for the management, the manager makes a demand for more salary, significantly more salary. The management, which has just had a difficult business year and is on an austerity course, rejects this demand. This is also because the manager is already well paid in the salary structure of the company as a whole. Since, in the eyes of the management, the manager came 'around the corner' with this demand completely unexpectedly, unprepared and without further explanation, the management also sees no need to explain itself and rejects the salary increase without further comment. The manager reacts angrily, openly threatening to leave the company. This would be a great loss for the management. The manager is in charge of two important projects and a successful team. However, the way the manager communicates displeases the management. They don't want to be threatened and react just as curtly: "Then just leave!".

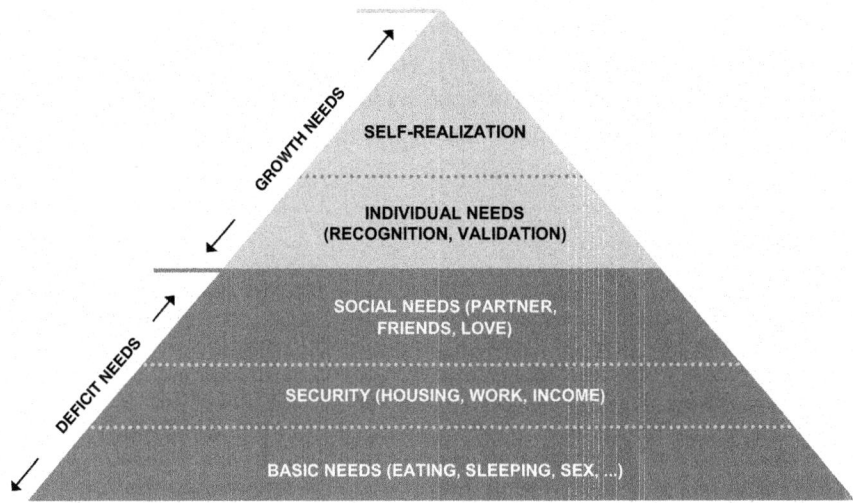

Fig. 4.1 The pyramid of needs according to Maslow

What happened here? In this conflict, positions were exchanged and no underlying interests were addressed. "I want more pay," is one position. "You don't get more pay," is a counter-position. The wanting-in this case, more pay-comes abruptly to the other side. They do not understand the position and react with incomprehension and curtness.

> **Example**
>
> *What management doesn't know is that the manager has specific needs that have triggered this demand. He is going through a difficult time in his personal life. His wife has separated from him. There is divorce and child support due. His assets are in a stock portfolio that has just swung mightily into the red and his liquidity is weak. However, since he has to move out of his home, he needs a deposit for the new apartment and money for furniture.*
>
> *His need for security is touched. Even though the manager is not a poor person per se, he lacks the resources he needs at this moment.*
>
> *However, the manager is too proud to bring this into the negotiation: "it's nobody's business". Management therefore only sees his position and could interpret: "the manager, who is already earning well, wants even more money". They too have a need behind the rejection of this demand: business is not good, the salary structure could be upset, it is not a good moment for a salary increase.*

If the two parties had already tried to exchange their needs behind the positions at this point, solutions might have been conceivable. The manager does not need more money in general, but just at this moment. Maybe the company could have offered him a favorable loan, maybe paying his bonus a little earlier would have been possible, etc. Transparency about the interests behind the position would have at least made mutual understanding possible. In this case, however, the demand has triggered a conflict.

> **Example**
>
> *The fronts harden. The rejection of his demand hits the manager, it touches another need: the need for appreciation. He feels unappreciated by the rejection and grumbles to his friends. "Now I do so much for this company year in, year out, wear myself out, spend my days late into the evening at the company, even sacrifice my marriage for work, and then when you get in need of something, you don't get it. I've had enough, I quit." Quitting was not at all originally in the manager's interest. Quitting entails considerable risks for him. The manager is almost 50 years old, it will not be so easy to find a suitably well-paid job and in a short time. The divorce also restricts his mobility; after all, he would like to see the children at the weekend.*

His positions: "Termination" is a 'want' that has arisen in conflict and has nothing to do with the original 'want', namely to get liquidity for a transitional period. It has taken on a life of its own. The management, who promptly react to the threat of termination, also expresses the position, 'then go ahead', without this corresponding to their actual interests. Their actual interest is the opposite of this (counter)position: they would have liked to keep the manager.

In a conflict, the will takes on a life of its own. The deeper we enter into the spiral of conflict, the more we distance ourselves from what we originally wanted, from our original needs. A desire, for example, that arises out of defiance and is based on the wish that the other person should not 'win' under any circumstances, overrides our original interests. In the course of a conflict it happens unnoticed that we lose sight of our interests, because of which the conflict once began. The change in wanting leads to fanaticism in the worst case. We blindly pursue positions that we vehemently defend, without these having been options for action in peaceful times.

The conflict has us firmly in its clutches. Our thinking, feeling and wanting has changed and has changed us. Our conflict partner experiences us as a changed personality and reacts accordingly. A dynamic arises that no longer has anything to do with the actual conflict of interests that underlies the dispute. The conflict controls us (Fig. 4.2).

Especially in separation situations, I always hear the irritated question: "I don't recognize my partner anymore. We have led a more or less happy

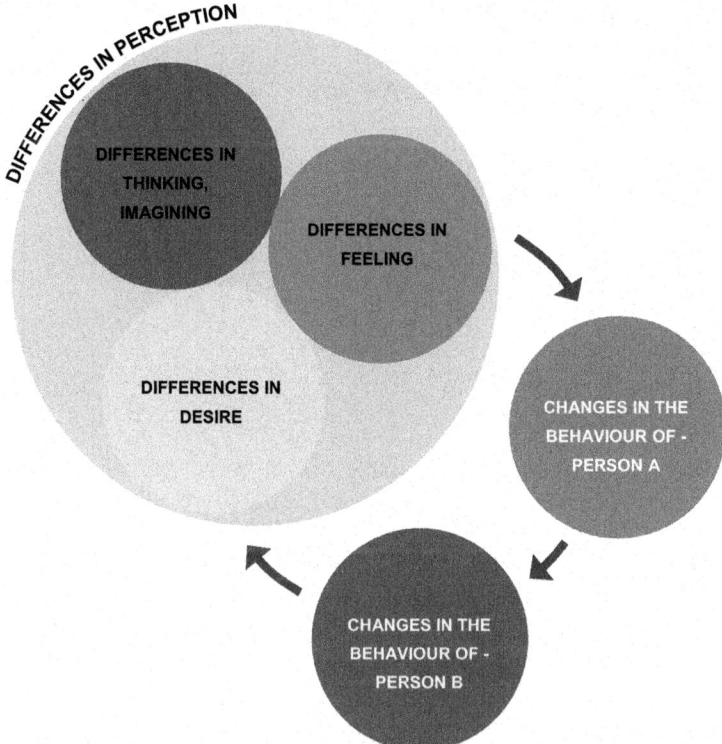

Fig. 4.2 Conflict spiral, loosely based on Friedrich Glasl

marriage for ten years, shared the bed and confided in each other the most secret thoughts and wishes, and now someone is sitting in front of me whose behavior is completely foreign to me – how could it come to this?" Once you understand the perceptual shift in the spiral of conflict, then they can give this distraught couple an answer. What is happening with this couple is the natural dynamic of people in escalated conflict.

And how do you get out of this spiral? That's what the next chapter is about.

5

Conflict Resolution

In this chap. I focus on the way out of the spiral of conflict. Making peace and moving out of the churning state of conflict into a calmer phase. Conflict resolution is usually understood to mean consensus-building techniques, such as mediation or clarification assistance. These are based on negotiating possible solutions and working out the agreements to keep the peace. This chapter is purely about getting out of the conflict spiral. This step is the basis for finding solutions and settling a conflict.

Let us think back again to the situation at the height of the conflict. The perception on the level of thinking, feeling and willing of the conflict parties has changed. This changed perception causes a change in action. The conflict parties do not recognise each other, the conflict stands before them as a threatening giant. It has long since ceased to be about the original issues. The conflict becomes a conflict about the conflict.

If one strives to clarify a conflict, then it is important to bring about clarification on the three levels of our perception. Thinking, feeling and wanting are not in a hierarchical relationship to each other; none of these levels is more important or less important than the other. In which category we first find explanatory approaches depends not least on our personality structure. For strongly analytical people, for example, clarification at the level of thinking tends to be more obvious and tangible than at the level of feeling. In a very emotional conflict, for example in the family, the category of feeling can be the first key to the turning point of the conflict.

Not every person who is in conflict has ever reflected on what that situation does to us. You, as the reader of this book, have already developed an understanding of the conflict dynamics of people. This knowledge helps us to better understand what is happening to us and our conflict partners in critical situations. I am always asked, as a conflict expert and mediator myself, if I have any conflicts at all. The answer is: of course I have conflicts. And of course I don't always react correctly in an argument. I experience destructive thought patterns and inappropriate behavior in myself when I am in conflict with someone. The difference from before is that I see and recognize exactly what I'm doing wrong and the dynamics I'm caught in somewhat delayed, as if on a parallel track. This doesn't necessarily help in the acute anger to change my own behavior, however in the aftermath I usually manage to look at what happened from a distance and sort out what behavior was conflict driven and focus on my original interests. In doing so, I have had to learn not to be too hard on myself and to allow myself, as well as everyone else, to make mistakes and get caught in the vortex of conflict. The goal is not to have no more conflict. When we remember the illusory giant Tur-Tur, who became the faithful companion of the two heroes of the novel, we also remember that conflict means development, and even painful conflict can certainly give us positive impulses for the rest of our lives. Avoiding conflicts is not the goal, but preventing the escalation of conflicts and the gradual alienation or even enmity with our conflict partners is worth striving for. First we look at ourselves: What can we do when we are caught in the vortex of an argument and we wish to end it? Let's try to focus on what seems possible at this moment of our own involvement. We go into self-clarification.

5.1 Self Clarification

The most effective way to get out of the conflict spiral is to become aware that we are in it. This sounds more mundane than it is. Much like people with addictions and dependencies that they don't (can't) admit to themselves, we are in the storm of conflict.

Since in this state we blame the other person, it is a great challenge to admit to ourselves that we too have changed our perception and behaviour in the conflict and that it is not only the other person who has become "strange". In order not to overwhelm ourselves, it is advisable to proceed gradually. It is best to find a quiet place, choose a quiet moment and stay completely with yourself for the time of the following self-reflections and reflections. As a reminder, we seek allies in conflict and desire loyalty from these 'conflict accomplices'. That is why it is important to take these first steps of reflection on our own behaviour, alone.

You can begin the reflection with one of the categories of our perception that changes in conflict: thinking, feeling, wanting.

Let's say you start with "the thinking":

To better understand how the relationship with our conflict partner has developed, it is helpful to create a timeline of the conflict. This timeline should be as accurate as possible.

For Example

Friday, March 13- during coffee break talking to my colleague- first point of contention about office seating arrangements.

Sunday, 15 March approx. 20.00 h – telephone call with colleague – subject: seating arrangements.

> **Important**
>
> The following questions can help you create such a timeline of the conflict:
>
> - When was the first disagreement?
> - At what point did they realize for themselves that they were in conflict?
> - When did you first start talking to others about the person(s) in conflict?
> - When did you first have strong feelings when thinking about the conflict (anger, sadness, rage, hurt, offended, etc.)?
> - Were there other events that fueled the conflict? When and what exactly?
> - Was there a time of relaxation? When was this?
> - When did you perceive a clear escalation? (A "point of no return": now the conflict has progressed so far that it cannot be pacified simply like that).
> - At what times were there disputes between them and the conflict partner(s)?
> - What other point in time is important in this history of conflict?

There is a methodical background to create such a timeline for yourself and.

very good to think about the order in which what happened: When our thinking changes in the conflict, it often goes hand in hand with the fact that we give different priorities to the order of events. The chronological order often recedes into the background and what particularly affected us or struck us is more present. When conflict participants tell the story of their conflict, we often hear in practice very different chronological sequences and contexts of events. Conflict partners accuse each other of distorting the facts and telling the untruth. However, this is not a conscious strategy, but an unconscious process. In self-reflection, the timeline and reflection on the course of the conflict in the next step helps us to understand the connection between action and reaction and to become aware of what in which phase of the dispute was the decisive factor in intensifying the conflict. By looking closely, we recognize patterns.

> **Example**
>
> For example, in a newly separated couple, the dispute always escalates when handing over the children after long holidays. Or in the case of two colleagues, there is a dispute when the boss is away on long business trips and not in the office.

In order to understand these patterns and the dynamics of the conflict and also the level of "feeling" more precisely, it is helpful to now look at the important stages of the conflict timeline in more detail. To do this, one writes next to the date what exactly happened, how I myself reacted, what the other person did in my eyes and what else seems important to me.

For Example

- *Friday, March 13- during coffee break talking to my colleague- first point of contention about office seating arrangements.*
- *It was about who is in favour of an open-plan office solution. I spoke out very clearly (and a bit heatedly) against my colleague's opinion. The other colleagues didn't say anything, but listened to us. My colleague also got louder and the tone between us was tense. My phone rang, so I left the round. We didn't speak to each other again all day. I was tense. So was she.*
- *Sunday, 15 March approx. 20.00 h- telephone call with colleague- subject: seating arrangements*
- *She called me to talk about our argument and to clarify the issue of seating arrangements. The conversation escalated, it was back to the open plan office issue. Her tone became sarcastic. I became louder. I hung up the phone in a rage. When I called again to apologize, she didn't answer. From that moment on, I was sure there was no quick resolution between us.*

What form these write-ups take is up to one's own taste and creativity. I have seen conflict lists in excel lists, as diary entries, and in the form of colorful painted posters and collages.

> **Important**
>
> A few questions can help structure your thoughts. Not all the questions listed here apply to all situations. Other questions may be relevant, so think about them and include them.
>
> - What exactly happened on this date?
> - What did I do or how did I react?
> - What was I thinking?
> - How did I feel?
> - How was I physically?
> - Who else was there?
> - What is the role of others at this point in the conflict?

If you have retraced the path of your conflict and looked thoroughly at the individual stages, you have already taken a first step out of the conflict spiral. Perhaps you have recognized patterns in your actions or thinking that repeat themselves on this rocky path. They are patterns of your conflict. Both conflict partners have their own patterns and a common pattern of conflict or escalation is formed by all participants.

> **Example**
>
> *Mrs. Bauer feels stressed after every discussion with Mrs. Wilhelm and then also reacts irritably to others. Reflecting on her conflict, she recognises this pattern: always after these discussions with Mrs Wilhelm, which are stressful for her, she has arguments with her children and her husband in the evening. The trigger of the argument in the evening is that her family is confronted with her bad mood and "does not want to hear something from this Mrs. Wilhelm again".*
>
> *Mrs. Wilhelm is also very upset by the discussions with her colleague. Afterwards, she regularly disappears into an earlier closing time, lies down on her bed at home and cries until she decides for herself, "Mrs. Bauer is not worth spoiling my life for". It's like a kind of mantra she uses to calm herself down.*
>
> *A common pattern of conflict, is the timing and setting of their discussion. Tension regularly builds up between them, and every 3–4 months it is released in one of these discussions. Often this happens when things are otherwise stressful in the office and everyone is busy. Actually an unfavorable time, as both reflect later, because in times of already increased stress, the burden of the conflict then takes on a peak.*

For self-exploration and reflection on their own actions, Mrs. Bauer and Mrs. Wilhelm could think about when exactly the conflict occurs and how these heated discussions come about? What are the so-called igniters? What actions or words cause this escalation? What is then said? How does the tone change? The better everyone understands in retrospect what he or she was thinking or originally wanted, the clearer the manipulation we experience in the conflict spiral. We understand better how the conflict affects thinking.

> **Important**
>
> In order to become aware of our own "feelings", it can also help here to go back on a timeline and consider how our feelings have changed over time. Or, for example, to create a map of conflicts, with ups and downs and different qualities of feeling.
> Guiding questions can be:
>
> - What feeling did I feel at the beginning of the conflict?
> - Were there any other feelings?
> - How have they changed over time?
> - Were there occasions that marked such a change?
> - Where do I feel the feelings?
> - How do I notice the feelings?

We do not have a rich vocabulary for expressing emotions, so it is important to explore the quality of the emotions we feel. One way to capture this is to observe where our emotions show up physically: *Does our throat feel rather constricted, do we have a heaviness in our chest, is our head under pressure, or do we feel dizzy.* There are many more such descriptions of sensations of strong feelings. When we go into self-reflection and create a map of our feelings, it is recommended that we also include the positive feelings that we either felt before the conflict or that we want to come back to. Even if it is nothing more than a wish at the moment of the conflict, focusing on something positive helps us to activate our resources and build a positive vision for the future. This has a motivating effect and people in conflict situations definitely need motivation.

The level of "wanting" also requires self-reflection. It is about my interests in this conflict and the needs associated with them. Caught in the spiral of conflict, our interests shift. What we originally wanted recedes into the background and it becomes important to us that, above all, the other person cannot assert his or her positions. It is therefore also important here to take a trip back in time and look back to the beginning of the dispute.

> **Important**
>
> In doing so, we can ask ourselves:
>
> - At the very beginning of the conflict, what did I want to do or not do, have or give?
> - What were my interests at the time and what was the need behind them?
> - How have my interests shifted over the course of the conflict?
> - What interests have become important to me now that I was not aware of before?
> - Which interests are particularly important to me today and which interests that I expressed in the conflict have lost their importance.

Conflicts can be resolved. The more precisely we know what we need in order to agree to a solution, the better it can be negotiated. In an escalated conflict, we often get stuck on one solution: *Either it goes my way, or I don't go along!*

Another helpful self-reflection in the case of conflict is therefore to think about *criteria* that a solution would have to fulfil in order for us to be able to engage in it. I would like to use an example to illustrate what is meant by *criteria for* a solution.

> **Example**
>
> *Ina wants to invite Jonas for a weekend trip. It is supposed to be a surprise. Ina and Jonas haven't known each other very long and Ina is nervous that she might pick something Jonas might not like. So she asked Jonas, "What do you think are important characteristics that you would use to determine whether a weekend getaway was successful?" Jonas thinks about it for a moment and answers, "There shouldn't be so many people around me so I can calm down. Good food is important to me and as much time as possible in the fresh air. I like The Mountains, whenever I've been there I feel like I've aired out."*
>
> *Ina can plan a weekend trip based on these characteristics: few people, quiet, good food, time in the fresh air and mountains. There are many ways to meet these criteria. Since she asked Jonas for criteria, she has the flexibility to surprise him. If she had asked Jonas which hotel or campsite he would like to go to and what program he would like there, the possible options would have been severely limited, a solution virtually predetermined and the surprise no longer surprising.*

In conflict we can do this exercise. In a thought experiment, we consciously discard the solutions we have already found that have not yet been heard by our conflict partner. Then, on a white sheet of paper, we consider criteria that good solutions must absolutely fulfil for us.

In doing so, we may think of criteria that, from our point of view, must be fulfilled in order for us to agree to a later solution and others that are perhaps not so important to us. The more open the criteria are, the better joint solutions can be found: e.g. *mountains and not the Alps or maintenance and not 2450 €*. In this way, we open up the scope for negotiation and enable new, joint and creative solutions.

Self-reflection means hard work. It provides us with surprising insights about ourselves – positive ones, but also dark, frightening ones. It is important to remain in resource activation and not to lose sight of the goal: to understand the conflict better and to find a way out of the conflict spiral.

Apart from internal conflicts, a conflict usually involves at least two people. Even if one of the participants reflects on the conflict, the question is pressing: What about the other conflict partners?

There are two broad directions:

- the others are also prepared to reflect on themselves and perhaps even engage in joint conflict resolution.
- the others refuse to work together on conflict resolution.

The first case is, you can guess, a favourable starting position. In my experience, the most important step towards conflict resolution is the recognition and willingness of both parties to want to pacify the conflict. In my opinion, this is also the reason why conflict resolution methods such as mediation achieve very high success rates (depending on the area of conflict, one assumes a conflict resolution rate of between 75% and 90%). The willingness to clarify one's conflict and the agreement of the conflict parties on a way of clarification, a method and a suitable moderator or mediator often arises from the desire to make peace. To finally dissolve the burden that has arisen from the conflict, perhaps over years, and in the future, to reshape the relationship. Which conflict clarifier is appropriate for which conflict may require consultation in some cases. My tip is to call a colleague who is a certified mediator without obligation, describe the conflict roughly and ask for a recommendation as to which resolution methods might be suitable. To be safe, it is advisable to talk to at least two mediators or conflict resolution experts. Conflict clarification requires openness and openness requires trust. If you decide to go the route of conflict clarification by means of a neutral third party, you should listen to your intuition after talking to providers and actively ask for the colleague's experience. In addition to professional clarifiers, there may be people in your environment who can take on the role of a mediator. In this case it is important that this person is neutral, accepted by all parties and is not part of the conflict themselves.

And of course you can also manage to clarify a conflict on your own! It is advisable to check the escalation of the conflict before attempting to clarify it. As a rule, the higher the conflict has escalated (see conflict levels), the more advisable it is for a neutral third party to accompany you. If the conflict is on the first three escalation levels (see conflict spiral), clarification is possible without outside help.

Unfortunately, there is also the case that the other person refuses to work together on conflict resolution. I am often asked by those affected what they can do then. Is it possible to step out of the conflict spiral all by yourself, even if the other person is still caught up in the dispute? Unfortunately, the answer is not clear-cut and applicable to all cases. It is yes:

Yes, it is possible to work on a conflict yourself and find your own way out of your conflict spiral. It is also possible to change the conflict dynamics by reflecting on one's own behaviour and the insights into what happens to us in a conflict. And yes, it often happens in this process of change that the conflict partner is suddenly willing to actively work on a clarification after all.

The no refers to the possibility of finding a common solution when an interlocutor completely refuses to communicate.

In the next chapter, I discuss what each person can do for themselves to understand the other.

5.2 Understanding the Others

Empathy, the ability to empathize with others, is lost in conflicts. In my experience, a great potential for conflict resolution lies in the restoration of this level. Only when we are prepared to want to understand the needs and the associated emotions of the other person, does a basis for conflict resolution emerge. Empathy is the basis of moral action. Lack of empathy is at the same time an inner license to act ruthlessly. The best way to establish empathy is for both to make an effort to pacify the conflict and to engage in a joint process. The willingness to clarify the conflict is not in itself sufficient to automatically "switch on" an understanding for the other person, but it is an important basis for changing the patterns established in the conflict. In a conversation with a conflict clarifier, for example a mediator, the gradual restoration of empathy usually takes place by directing the conversation towards the interests and needs and the associated emotions of the conflict parties. At best, the mediator does not let up at this point and continues to ask about the interests behind the parties' formulated positions until he or she feels that the parties' own interests have been worked out and understood. There are various techniques in mediation to achieve this.

Without a neutral conflict mediator but with the willingness of both to pacify the conflict, the restoration of empathy succeeds in a similar way. In a dispute conversation we often work with positions that are solidified over time and often repeated like a prayer wheel. We have already seen the difference between position and interest in the case of the manager who needed a raise.

> **Example**
>
> *Another example is Mr and Mrs Meier. They are newly separated and have two children. The conflict is mainly about the care times of the children: Mr. Meier would like to see the children every other weekend and two days a week. Mrs. Meier is on the position of "every other weekend and no more days". They have been insisting on these positions of weekend + 2 and weekend + 0 for months. Neither of them deviates from their position and neither of them really understands why the other one insists on this position.*

One aspect of why disputants insist on a position lies in the fact that they interpret giving in as a "win" for the other. This is what they want to avoid. Remember, in the escalation of a conflict we prefer not to assert our original interests as long as the other person does not assert his interests either and does not "win". At some point, we don't even care about our interests and all we care about is that the other person loses, even at the cost of us losing in the process.

The other aspect in the struggle for positions is that the parties do not clarify their interests behind their positions. For example, we represent positions such as, *every other weekend and no day more,* where we have our own interests, not fully reflected. We have then adopted this position, for example, because it is a counter-position to our conflict partner or because such a model is also practiced by our neighbor and we only know this one. Or this position is based on interests which we have reflected on, but which we do not want to express because they are perhaps unpleasant to us or we do not feel safe to reveal ourselves. In a clarifying conflict conversation, this step is essential. Only if we ourselves know our interests and formulate them openly to our interlocutor and name the associated feelings, do we have a chance that this openness and transparency will trigger a response in the other person in the form of a budding empathy. Naming interests is a necessary step in finding good solutions. Good solutions should take into account as many of the interests of all partners as possible.

Example

Mrs. Meier formulates her interests behind the position weekend + 0. One aspect is particularly difficult for her to formulate. Mrs. Meier was left by her husband and still suffers a lot from the separation. Seeing her ex-husband causes her great pain. One reason why she pursues the position weekend + 0 so vehemently is that she wants to minimize the contact points of handing over the children to the father. As she feels very great sadness after the handovers and has to expend a lot of energy to get back on track. She also formulates that her interest is not to deprive the children of their father, as she knows how important he is for the children and that he is a good father.

This openness to express your interest required a lot of strength and overcoming from Mrs. Meier. The need behind this is self-protection.

Mr. Meier did not expect that his ex-wife still suffers so much from the separation. Now he understands better how this attitude could have come about. Until now, he has assumed that his ex-wife's aim was to withhold the children from him. He sees how emotional his ex-wife is about this issue and how much energy the negotiation is costing her. He develops a sense of compassion. The solution the two end up with was based on both of their interests. In order to minimize contact, at least for the next few months, as long as Mrs. Meier has this feeling of sadness in her, the two agreed that the children would not visit their father two extra days during the week, but would stay with him on each of his weekends from Thursday evening to Monday evening.

It requires courage and honesty with oneself and the other person to formulate the interests. Important here is the way in which the interests and needs are formulated.

A conversation technique that is also used in non-violent communication is the "I" and "You" messages. In conflict communication, the "you messages" predominate.

Background Information

For example, a "you message" sounds like this: *"You always come home late at night and don't take care of the kids, it all gets stuck with me. You get on my nerves!"*

As a "I message" it would sound like this: *"I wish you wouldn't come home too late in the evening and then help take care of the kids. I feel overwhelmed when I have to take this on alone in the evening and it makes me angry. I wish I had support from you."*

The difference lies in the fact that the first message contains reproaches. Positions are formulated here to which the person addressed will automatically react with a counter-position. The person addressed feels attacked and counterattacks or withdraws, depending on the individual type of conflict. Both actions, however, do not lead to constructive communication about the interests that lie behind the statement: here – the desire for support and for appreciation.

With the "I-message", the self-revelation is in the foreground. "I wish…" is an important sentence. The focus is not on the reproach of what has not happened or occurred, but on the wish of what could happen or become different. In doing so, it is important with "I messages" to express the emotion associated with the need. In this case, *"I feel overwhelmed and it makes me angry"*. The more concretely the interest is named: "I am asking for your support", "I want help/attention", etc., the better the other person can understand what is being said. The more precisely the participants understand the emotions involved, the better they are able to put themselves in the other person's shoes and develop empathy.

This open exchange about interests and the needs and emotions behind them touches the areas of feeling and wanting. This is a two-way process. Just as important as making our interests understood is that we understand the interests and needs of the other.

> **Important**
> The best way to do that is to ask for it directly:
>
> - What is particularly important to you at this point?
> - What is your need, behind this demand?
> - What interest do you have in doing/not doing/changing that?
> - What feelings are associated with it?
> - What would happen if nothing changed? How would you feel then?

In order to understand as precisely as possible what the other person is talking about and at the same time to give the other person the signal of full attention, the technique of "active listening" can be used. It is crucial to stay in the present moment of the conversation. To focus on what the other person is saying without distraction. This concentration on the interlocutor can be expressed by looking into the eyes of the interlocutor and making it clear, for example with a nod of the head or approving sounds such as mmh, yes, aha, etc., that one's senses are completely focused on what the other person is saying. This "visible" concentration on the interlocutor encourages him or her to continue. Active listening shows an appreciation for the other person's openness. Internally, the challenge is to take what is said as it is said. To listen and not immediately interpret or develop parallel rebuttals in one's mind. This is easier said than done. We immediately develop our own opinions when listening, not only in conflict conversations, but in almost any communication. With very communicative people, this can be a strong reflex to immediately counter something, to contribute something. The focus then shifts away from listening and concentrating on the other person. I put myself in the foreground when I immediately think of my own story about what has just been said. An experience, an idea, a rebuttal already sitting in my mouth, impatiently waiting to come out as soon as the other person is finished. Interlocutors sense this and feel not heard and certainly not understood. With inwardly turned people, this often happens inside without them saying everything thought out loud right away. The effect, however, is similar, even after a short time of a conversation, they become preoccupied with their own thoughts instead of listening first. In a conflict conversation, listening is an important signal to our conflict partner and a method to understand better. When we listen consciously and show it, it is very different from the destructive communication that prevails in conflicts. The other person will be positively surprised, he or she will appreciate and acknowledge this and feel heard for the first time in a long time. Feeling heard is the first step to feeling understood.

The second stage of active listening is that we ask questions. Comprehension questions if we have not understood what has been said or deepening questions if we have not yet grasped the interest behind the positions or have not yet heard how our conversation partner actually feels. These questions should be asked in a non-confrontational manner, especially in a conflict situation. As soon as the interlocutor feels verbally backed into a corner or feels that the questions are rhetorical in nature with no expectation of genuine interest in the answer, the atmosphere of the conversation is violated. Genuine interest and questions that lead to a better understanding of the other person trigger in our counterpart the feeling of being better understood and of being able to open up.

The final stage of active listening and is summarizing what has been said – also called paraphrasing. This is not about repeating everything the other person has said. However, in the case of critical or complicated issues, it is a good idea to repeat what has been said in your own words to make sure that you have understood everything correctly.

Background Information

For example, after a dialogue between the two spouses about the children's residency arrangements, *"Did I understand you correctly that the reason you don't want to do the weekend + 2 model is because then we'll have frequent child surrenders and it still takes a toll on you emotionally when you see me?"*

Here the interlocutor can either agree: *"Yes, that's true. That's what I meant"* or add something else, in this case for example *"Yes, I'm still not over our breakup and every encounter makes me very sad and it takes a lot of energy to get me out of this hole again"*.

These loops in the dialogues help to create a better and deeper understanding. It takes some practice to reproduce what a conversation partner has said. It is advisable to summarise smaller units rather than whole conversations at the end. I should summarize what I have heard and not what I have interpreted myself. One rule is to always ask for reassurance that what I have understood and just summarised is actually what I meant. This process creates constructive communication, a deeper understanding of each other and the basis for the development of empathy. In the process, what was originally intended also slips back into the focus of the conversation.

But what if the other person refuses and is not ready for a clarifying conversation? Breaking out of the conflict spiral on your own requires courage, strength and self-discipline. While the perception of the other person is in conflict mode, we try to de-escalate the dispute with constructive communication. We have already taken the first step by self-reflecting on our conflict dynamics and perhaps recognizing patterns that we would like to break in the future. For example, *"when she yells, I don't yell too"*. This change in behavior, affects the overall dynamics of the conflict and will cause irritation in the conflict partner who is not yet ready to actively engage with the conflict dynamics. Constructive behaviour in an escalated conflict is not necessarily welcomed by the other party. In the consistency of our conflict thinking, it disturbs us when the other person, for example, suddenly keeps quiet in our otherwise very loud arguments. It can cause the conflict spiral to turn a little further for our conflict partner. Our changed behaviour is usually not interpreted positively, but as a ruse, as manipulation or a pretence. Now we need patience to show the other person that we are serious about constructive communication. Changing the "you messages" into "I messages" is crucial. When given the opportunity, it is helpful to explain our interests behind our positions. We can't expect these needs and associated emotions to be picked up by the other person right away. This requires patience and perseverance, and reflection that the other person or persons are in a state of conflict where empathy is not possible. The opportunity, however, is that our changed behavior fundamentally changes the dynamics of the conflict. Behavior is reciprocal. The provocations, spikes and mutual injuries, are no longer answered by us with just that. They are mirrored, in which we express how much we are hurt by what is being said and what we actually wanted to discuss when we approached him or her. Usually, after some time, steady de-escalating behavior changes the dynamic between the disputants and opens a window of readiness for conflict resolution in the other person. This one-sided de-escalation requires a lot of strength, inner clarity and patience.

And what if the other person doesn't want to talk to us at all? This also happens again and again in conflicts. The communication is broken off. All well-intentioned attempts to pick it up again fail. In such a situation, it is useless to chase after the other person and beg, plead, rage for him to talk to us. Communication and conflict resolution are always self-determined and voluntary. As much as it hurts, we cannot force someone to talk to us if he or she refuses. We are alone with ourselves. There remains the possibility to work on all conflict-relevant topics that one can clarify or clear up with oneself. To recognize one's own patterns, to work out one's own interests, needs and emotions for oneself. And to say goodbye to that conflict being pacified. Letting go, grieving and emotionally detaching from the issue and the person connected to it as much as possible are healing steps.

Turning the conciliatory gaze to the good of the conflict and the lessons learned. What did this conflict show me about myself? What did I realize about my patterns of thinking, acting and feeling in the conflict and how can I do it differently in similar, recurring situations?

Once you have resolved yourself internally and perhaps even made peace with the fact that this conflict will not be resolved, you are not infrequently surprised by the fact that the possibility of communication suddenly and unexpectedly opens up. Typically after major changes in one's life, such as having children, divorce, death of a loved one, serious illness, joyful graduation, promotion at work, unemployment, corona lock down and similar cutbacks, our view of what is important and unimportant in our lives changes. Priorities shift. Unresolved conflicts either seem particularly burdensome in the face of major life changes and the motivation to throw this ballast overboard increases, or they seem so banal in the presence of external "catastrophes" that one wonders why the fronts are actually too hardened and whether this pain is worth it. And so it happens again and again, surprisingly, that people who have reacted to conflicts by breaking off contact pick up the thread of communication again. In this case, the gate to the abandoned conflict spiral is wide open.

5.3 Making Peace

Making peace sounds big. Most people associate peace with war.

Even though most conflicts fortunately do not involve total annihilation by force of arms, the disputants in the eye of the conflict spiral find themselves in a stressful state of emergency. You have read in the last chapters how it is possible to leave this unpleasant cycle. Only when the parties to the conflict change their perception towards normality does a basis for finding a solution emerge. These joint determinations have the function of a contract. It may be necessary to actually negotiate a contract with the help of lawyers and notaries. In other cases, a verbal agreement is sufficient. The purpose is to secure peace at the moment and in the future. The fine art of finding a solution is to reach a consensus. Consensus, which was described in detail in Chap. 3, should be recalled here. It is achieved when all important interests of the negotiating partners are taken into account. Those who succeed in finding a consensus have a good chance of this solution being sustainable and accepted and embraced by all parties. Finding a consensus often requires creative solutions:

> **Example**
> *Dominik plays with the red car and Ina also wants to play with the red car. But there is only one red car. There is a lot of bickering. In order to create a consensus here, inventiveness is needed. Dominik and Ina are creative. The red car gets a special status. A pedestal is built and the car is exhibited. It is the mascot of the self-built city and all other cars drive around it. No one is allowed to touch the red car but both are allowed to admire it.*

Sometimes, however, a conflict is not about a negotiated or even contractual solution at all. Especially in social conflicts, when the topic is about appreciation, recognition, trust or respect, the focus is not on reaching an agreement at the end. What should it be? "*Today, I want appreciation from you twice a day,*" or "*Starting tomorrow at 12:00, trust me 90% again*"? These conflicts are about gaining an understanding from the other person about their own needs. The lack of understanding that leads to the conflict may have arisen, for example, through misunderstanding, carelessness or even through different cultural socialisation and the associated expectations and wishes. The conflict is then a process of negotiation based on mutual understanding. It is not a solution at the end that is decisive, but the depth, sincerity and openness of the confrontation and the degree to which it has been possible to develop mutual understanding.

Whether the path of conflict is the goal or an agreement marks the end of conflict, it is advisable to make peace after any conflict: Conflict resolution is a lengthy and energy-consuming process of change. Just as the conflict has suddenly appeared and a starting point exists, it should also have an end. Making peace is important to mark that end. The conflict is over, new times are dawning. These new times are not the continuation of old peaceful times after great conflicts. Conflict has left its mark, it has changed us. The times of peace that are now beginning are different.

Peace means the absence of disturbance or alarm. Signs of peace and rituals of pacification exist across all cultures. Peace pipe, peace doves, peace dances, communal peace festivals are just a few. These rituals help to consolidate the state that has been reached. A commitment of the participants to the jointly achieved agreement is created. We know from commitment research that the likelihood of pursuing resolutions increases considerably when the participants consciously commit to them. The explanation is that we are anxious to do what we said we would do. But this is again the psychological principle of consistency. It has the power to drive human action and is consistently described as one of the central psychological motives. Research concludes that we strive for consistency in our actions and appearances, and that this striving leads us to do things that we are not aware of or that we would not do without the existing mechanism of consistency. We have already learned about the principle in the behavioral change of people in conflict.

Most people have a need to be and appear consistent in their words, beliefs, and actions. This tendency to be consistent feeds primarily from three sources: Consistency is highly valued in society, has worked well in everyday life (avoiding the back-and-forth of too many small decisions), and provides a kind of fast-track that makes it easier to deal with the complexity of modern life.

Social psychology describes the trigger of the influence of consistency on our human actions in commitment, or attachment to something. Once one has adopted a point of view, there is a tendency to remain consistent with that point of view.

A commitment once made has an influence on the self-image if it was made actively and voluntarily. One method to create consistency is to formulate a commitment.

The consistency pressure on the self-image of a commitment, once established, exists on two levels. Internally, there is the effort to bring the self-image in line with one's own actions; and externally, we feel the pressure to conform this image to the view others have of us.

When making peace, it is therefore crucial how consciously and intensively this gesture is performed. I consciously encourage conflict parties to perform this ritual. It can be an extensive handshake, a hug, a long eye-to-eye look, a joint letter, a joint meal, a walk, burying the conflict box, a fire of old burdens, a gift. I have been able to experience many variations in my practice. It is important that all parties involved in the conflict feel comfortable with it and that the gesture is carried out consciously and not casually or incidentally and that it is sincere. Even the joint search for the appropriate "peace ceremony" is a moment of lightness. The focus moves away from conflict and what was to something new, the sealing of peace. I encourage you to consciously mark the end of conflicts at work as well. It doesn't have to be grand gestures, a genuine handshake, a shared meal and a spoken commitment to the solution found, already stabilize the agreement.

Only when we have found peace do we appreciate our conflicts as sources of change. And only when we have walked in the spiral of conflict do we know the soothing calm of the state of peace.

Printed by Printforce, United Kingdom